THE KITCHEN CEO

A Practical Guide to Getting Seen, Stocked, and Sold in Today's Food Retail Landscape

Part Two of The Food Founders Series: A Focus on Your Placement & Promotion

Book 2

CRYSTAL M. BLACK-DAVIS

Contents

Industry Frameworks and Methodologies Disclaimer

The Kitchen CEO series references a wide range of business principles, operational practices, financial concepts, retail methodologies, marketing frameworks, and industry terminology commonly used throughout the consumer packaged goods (CPG), grocery, manufacturing, foodservice, and retail industries. These concepts were not created or invented by the author, nor are they presented as original proprietary intellectual property.

Rather, this series represents the author's interpretation, sequencing, organization, and explanation of broadly recognized industry knowledge accumulated through nearly two decades of professional experience working within the packaged food and beverage industry across brand management, retail, distribution, strategy, marketing, manufacturing, and commercialization. Many of the formulas, frameworks, systems, and operational concepts discussed throughout these books have roots in established business theory, economics, retail operations, supply chain management, finance, marketing, and organizational strategy developed over many decades by researchers, institutions, corporations, educators, and industry practitioners.

Because many modern business and CPG concepts have evolved

collectively across industries over time, it is often difficult or impossible to attribute every individual term, methodology, or operational practice to a single original source or creator. However, the author has made a good-faith effort to identify and acknowledge widely recognized frameworks, organizations, standards bodies, and foundational business concepts within the "Sources, Frameworks, and Industry References" section included in the back matter of this book.

The purpose of this series is educational and practical in nature: to help founders, entrepreneurs, and emerging operators better understand the often complex realities of the food and consumer packaged goods industries through clear explanations, real-world context, and industry-informed guidance. Any trademarks, standards, methodologies, organizational names, or referenced frameworks remain the intellectual property of their respective owners and are referenced solely for educational, commentary, and informational purposes.

Introduction

Since relaunching Savvy Food Consulting in 2020, I've worked with numerous founders eager to turn their culinary ideas into packaged products. Some came with restaurant experience, others from entirely different industries, healthcare, education, and even tech. They were passionate, hardworking, and successful in their own right. But what they almost universally lacked was an understanding of the business of food.

An overwhelming number of the founders I encountered had no prior exposure to grocery retail. No sense of how pricing is structured, what distributors actually do, or that products are often reviewed only once, sometimes twice a year for inclusion on grocery shelves. They built their projections using generic business templates that didn't account for trade spend, historically slow payment terms, and deductions that can make or break cash flow.

The result? Many were underbudgeted, misforecasted, and overextended before they even had the chance to scale.

That's why I wrote *The Kitchen CEO*.

The Kitchen CEO is a three-book series designed to pull back the curtain on the food CPG industry and help founders build businesses that are not only launch ready but built to last. Each book focuses on a critical pillar of a successful food company, guiding founders from product development and pricing to distribution and promotion, and finally to building the people, systems, and plans required for sustainable growth.

Book Two shifts the focus from readiness to results. Once a product reaches retail, success is no longer defined by access alone, but by performance. Placement and promotion determine whether a product earns attention, drives repeat purchases, and justifies its space on shelf. This book explores how brands translate a solid foundation into real-world traction, where distribution choices and marketing investments must work in tandem to support growth that lasts.

At this stage, visibility becomes a business decision. Whether you're preparing for your first retail rollout or navigating early regional distribution, the way your product is introduced, supported, and sustained in-store matters as much as the product itself. Book Two is about approaching that visibility with intention, understanding not just where your product appears, but how it competes once it's there.

Rather than relying on assumptions or guesswork, this book pulls back the curtain on retail execution. You'll learn how buyers evaluate categories, how promotions are planned and funded, and why metrics like velocity and sell-through carry more weight than door count alone. Each chapter is designed to help you anticipate expectations, reduce costly missteps, and work more effectively with retailers, distributors, brokers, and marketing partners by speaking the shared language of the industry.

My Approach

When I switched from tech marketing to the food industry two decades ago, I was amazed by how much happened behind the curtain. The grocery aisle seemed simple on the surface, but the elements that powered it proved to be anything but. That initial assumption has been a stumbling block for so many founders.

When I relaunched Savvy post-COVID, my business was tailored to consulting imported food CPG brands and raw ingredient suppliers on U.S. market readiness. Despite that specific customer focus, I started receiving requests from domestic startup and early-stage food brand founders seeking help with their rollouts. During those conversations, I noticed something striking: founders were eager to learn, but the tools available to them were inadequate. They were utilizing one-size-fits-all, generic business plan templates that didn't reflect the distinct nuances of food CPG. Relying on industry-agnostic plans can and has led to serious miscalculations in budgets, inventory, and forecasting.

That problem formed *The Kitchen CEO* series.

These books intend to share the industry knowledge I've gained since 2006. To make transparent what's often treated as insider information. I want you to understand how costs stack up in distribution, what buyers expect from manufacturers, how to understand syndicated data, and why forecasting errors can quietly sink even the most promising brand.

Throughout this books, you'll find:

- **Realistic frameworks** drawn from actual retail practices, not startup theory.

- **Simulated examples** that show both success and missteps, because we learn from both.

- **Tools and templates** to help you calculate, plan, and project like an industry insider.

- **Straight talk** about costs, margins, and capacity, because optimism is no substitute for preparation.

My commitment is to help you build a business plan rooted in clarity and credibility. One that reflects how this industry truly works, not how entrepreneurs (and investors) wish it did.

By the end of *The Kitchen CEO* series, my goal is that you'll not only understand how to build a viable food business, but you'll also be able to articulate your numbers, strategy, and vision with the confidence of someone who's already operating in the industry.

Who The Kitchen CEO Is For

The Kitchen CEO was written for anyone interested in turning a food idea into a viable, scalable business, especially those who want to do it the *informed* way.

It's for the founder who has perfected a family recipe, received rave reviews at local farmers markets, and now wants to know what it will take to reach store shelves.

It's for the early-stage entrepreneur preparing to raise funds or approach distributors, who realizes that enthusiasm and a tasty product won't replace the need for solid financials, strategic pricing, and operational discipline.

It's also for the career shifter entering the food industry from another field. Someone with drive, creativity, and applicable skills, but lacks an insider's view of how grocery retail really works.

Additionally, it's for consultants, investors, and advisors who want to understand the actual dynamics of this industry so they can better evaluate opportunities and set realistic forecasts.

No matter where you are in your journey, dreaming, planning, launching, or scaling, *The Kitchen CEO* will help you build a smarter, stronger foundation for your food business.

All About Me

Hello, I'm Crystal Black-Davis, a seasoned food industry executive (pun intended), strategist, and advisor with two decades of experience leading brand growth, market expansion, and strategic development for some of the world's most beloved consumer packaged goods (CPG) brands in top retailers.

In 2006, I founded Savvy Food Marketing, a boutique consultancy dedicated to helping imported food and beverage companies navigate the complex path from shipping container to the pantries of U.S. consumers. My sharp industry insight and results-oriented approach soon caught the attention of the global confectionery brand Loacker, initially hiring me as a marketing consultant and, in 2014, as a full-time employee, Vice President of Marketing. In a little over a year, I was promoted to Executive Vice President of Loacker USA, where I oversaw business development, U.S. innovation, and national retail expansion, driving multi-million-dollar growth and establishing partnerships with major retailers including Target, Whole Foods, and Eataly.

I relaunched my firm as Savvy Food Consulting in 2020, reflecting my broadened expertise and deepened commitment to supporting both packaged and raw ingredient food businesses.

Today, my team and I help brands, investors, and retail partners develop strategies that combine market insight, consumer understanding, and operational precision, bridging the gap between creative vision and commercial success.

I have worked with a diverse portfolio of customers, guiding them through pricing, positioning, retail readiness, and sustainable growth planning. My ability to translate industry complexity into clear, actionable strategies has made me a trusted advisor across the sector.

Food isn't just my profession and favorite pastime, it was also the focus of my academic studies. I hold a Master's degree in Gastronomy with a concentration in Food Policy from Boston University, and I'm a graduate of Cornell University's Food Industry Management Executive Program.

Through my consulting work, speaking engagements, and now *The Kitchen CEO*, I am committed to democratizing knowledge and access for founders from all walks of life and launch stages.

I live in the New York City metro with my husband and son, balancing a wonderful life steeped in food, family, and culture.

In food CPG, success isn't just about having a great product…
it's about having a great plan.

-Crystal Black-Davis

Your Why

Before the spreadsheets, the sell sheets, and the shelf placements, there's *your why*.

Every founder has one. It's the reason you're willing to risk your comfort, your savings, your time, and quite possibly, your sanity to bring a food product into the world. Maybe it started as a family recipe that everyone urged you to package and sell. Maybe it's an innovative solution to a health challenge, a cultural cuisine you're proud to share, or a better-for-you version of something you've always loved.

Whatever your reason, it's the heartbeat of your business.

Many founders have their *what* and their *how*, but their *why* isn't clearly defined or aligned with the realities of building a sustainable food CPG company.

Launching a food brand is not just about getting on store shelves; it's about building something that reflects your values, your story, and the needs of your consumers. Your *why* will be the anchor when challenges hit, when funding feels tight, and when progress moves slower than you imagined.

So take this moment to ask yourself:

- Why am I truly pursuing this business?
- Why is *now* the right time to launch?
- What change do I want to create in the market?
- What consumer demand am I meeting?
- What will success mean to me, beyond sales?

Be honest with yourself. Clarity here will shape the decisions that follow, how you price your product, choose your partners, and define growth.

Your *why* is the foundation of your business. It's the quiet conviction that keeps you going long after the novelty fades.

Write it down. Refine it. Return to it often. Because when your *why* is clear, every *how* becomes easier to build.

A Focus on Placement and Promotion

Once your product and pricing are solid, the next step is to ensure that the right people can find, experience, and remember your brand. Book 2 of *The Kitchen CEO* centers on Placement and Promotion, the two forces that determine how your product moves through the market and how your story connects with consumers. These are the areas where strategic visibility meets emotional resonance, where data-driven decisions merge with creative execution.

Placement is more than just where your product sits on a shelf. It's about access, availability, and alignment. The channels you choose, whether grocery, specialty, natural, club, or e-commerce, each come with their own expectations, buyers, and rhythms. Understanding how the supply chain works, how distributors operate, and how category managers think allows you to navigate retail with confidence. Strategic placement isn't just about distribution; it's about distribution that makes sense for your brand stage, your target consumer, and your cash flow. A well-placed product can outperform competitors with larger budgets simply by being in the right stores, at the right time, and in the right way.

Promotion, on the other hand, is how you build momentum. It's where awareness becomes action. In the crowded landscape of food and beverage CPG, consumers are bombarded with choices, and your message must cut through the noise. From digital storytelling and influencer partnerships to in-store demos and trade promotions, every touchpoint should reinforce who you are and why your product matters. Effective promotion builds credibility, drives trial, and creates loyal advocates both at the trade and consumer level.

Together, placement and promotion determine how the market perceives your brand. One ensures your product is physically present; the other ensures it's emotionally and mentally present. This book will help you understand how to approach distributors, plan trade shows, manage your retail footprint, and create marketing campaigns that connect with purpose. By mastering these two P's, you move beyond simply being *on the shelf,* you become part of the consumer's world.

How This Book Series Was Built

In 2022, I began revisiting the numerous files I had accumulated throughout my career, notes from buyer meetings, go-to-market plans, distributor agreements, trade show contracts, research queries, business plans, pricing models, etc. As I sifted through those documents, I started outlining what would become *The Kitchen CEO*. I realized that much of what I had learned lived in fragments across years of experience, conversations, and relationships. The book series grew from that process of reflection and reconstruction. The insights shared here are grounded in that practical, operational reality.

The food CPG industry functions on a set of shared understandings that are often unspoken. Trade economics, buyer expectations, slotting structures, velocity benchmarks, and promotional standards are not obvious concepts; they are elusive structures that shape outcomes. Founders who enter this space without visibility into these dynamics frequently learn through costly trial and error. That realization became the catalyst for the books. I wanted to make the invisible visible. I wanted entrepreneurs to walk into this industry informed, steady, and confident rather than guessing their way forward.

During the writing process, I used several tools, including artificial intelligence platforms, to help organize ideas, test clarity, and refine drafts. These technologies functioned as professional tools, similar to financial modeling software or data visualization apps. They supported clarity and efficiency but did not originate the insights contained in the series. All interpretations, recommendations, and perspectives reflect my vast professional experience, informed by two decades spent deep in the trenches.

The Kitchen CEO Mindset

Launching a food company is not for the faint of heart. It requires resilience, clarity, and the willingness to learn faster than you ever have before.

The *Kitchen CEO Mindset* is the combination of perspective and discipline that allows entrepreneurs to navigate uncertainty with confidence. It's what separates those who *start* a food business from those who *build* one that lasts.

In the early days, you'll wear every hat: CEO, marketer, salesperson, accountant, and sometimes delivery driver. It's easy to feel scattered or reactive. The goal isn't to eliminate those moments but to manage them with intention. A founder who understands both the art *and* the architecture of their business will be better prepared for the realities ahead, ingredient shortages, production errors, delayed purchase orders, or unexpected chargebacks.

The right mindset starts with four pillars:

Curiosity and Humility

You'll never know it all. And as odd as this may sound, use that to your advantage. The food industry changes constantly: consumer

tastes, retailer priorities, ingredient costs, and compliance requirements all evolve. Stay curious. Ask questions. Talk to retailers,
distributors, and other founders. Humility keeps you open to advice;
receptivity turns that advice into action.

Resilience and Realism

Every founder faces rejection, buyers who say "not right now,"
retailers who pass, or distributors who don't return your calls. What
matters is how you respond. Resilience allows you to stay the course,
but realism ensures you pivot when needed. Many food brands fail
not for lack of passion but for ignoring data, inventory trends, and
cash flow realities.

Strategic Patience

It's tempting for founders to pursue every new opportunity. "Swing
as many doors," as they say. But not every opportunity is good for
your brand. Timing and capacity are often the top factors when
assessing new opportunities. I've seen many instances where large,
unfillable purchase orders serve as a detriment, not a benefit, to
founders. Growth should be strategic, not reactionary. The most
successful founders know when to pause, reassess, and scale in a way
that preserves both capital and brand integrity.

Purpose and Accountability

Your *why* and your *what* will only take you so far if your *how* isn't
grounded in integrity. Accountability, both to yourself and your
partners, builds credibility. Deliver on your promises, communicate
transparently, and remember that every retailer, broker, and
consumer interaction shapes how your brand is perceived.

Checking In With the Founders

Following How Our Founders Move From Product Readiness to Market Reach

In Book One, each of our founders built the foundation of a viable food product. They identified their purpose, refined their recipes, calculated their true COGS, validated pricing, and learned what it means to bring a food item to life with intention. Now, as we enter Book Two, they stand at the threshold of a new challenge: getting their product into the world through the right channels, with the right strategies, and at the right time. Placement and promotion require a different kind of discipline, one rooted in visibility, relationship-building, and strategic execution. Here's where each founder stands as the next chapter of their journey begins.

Elena - Harbor Harvest Foods
(Spiced Mango Preserves)

Ready to Step Beyond the Market Table

Elena enters this next phase with excitement and clarity. After refining her MVP and validating her concept through farmers markets and small-batch production, she knows that consumers respond to her handcrafted sauces and to the authenticity of her story. Now she's ready to expand, but in a controlled, thoughtful way. Her focus turns to identifying the right first stores, understanding how wholesale pricing works, and learning the mechanics of distribution. She wants to build awareness without overextending her budget, and Book Two will show her how to take her first steps into retail with both confidence and care.

Marcus - Summit Sips (Clean
Labeled Sparkling Iced Tea)

Strategizing His Route to Regional Retail

Marcus approaches his next chapter with the mindset of a strategist. His well-funded, data-informed brand has strong margins and scalable production, but Book One reminded him that numbers alone don't guarantee market success. Now he's ready to translate his planning into purposeful action. He's thinking about which regions to enter first, how retailers evaluate brands, and how to build promotional programs that align with his sales goals. His challenge is not whether he can scale, but how to scale responsibly. Book Two will help him refine the systems that turn ambition into sustainable growth.

Danielle - Bountiful Bites (Upcycled Snacks)

Returning With Hard-Earned Clarity

For Danielle, this new phase marks a second chance, one grounded in humility and informed decision-making. Her earlier launch attempt struggled because she overcommitted before understanding the financial and operational realities outlined in Book One. After rebuilding her product and pricing model, she is approaching the market with a cautious, intentional mindset. She wants to re-enter through smaller, lower-risk placements and craft promotions that protect her margin instead of eroding it. Book Two gives her the tools to design a measured comeback, one rooted in clarity rather than urgency.

Andre - Kindred Grains
(Ancient Grain Snacks)

Preparing for a Wiser Second Launch

Andre enters Book Two wiser and more disciplined than ever. His first brand struggled under the weight of rapid expansion, weak margins, and an underdeveloped promotional strategy, all pitfalls he now recognizes clearly after completing Book One. This time, he's determined to start smart. As he prepares for his second launch, he is focused on choosing channels that fit his capacity, crafting thoughtful trade stories, rebuilding retailer relationships, and ensuring that his operations can support the placements he's pursuing. Book Two offers him the structural understanding he lacked in his first venture, and he's ready to put those lessons into practice.

The Founders Enter the Next Phase

Together, these founders embody the range of realities entrepreneurs face as they transition from developing a product to preparing it for the market. Their goals differ, their paths vary, and their resources are not the same, but they share a common moment: their products are ready, and now it's time to make them visible. Book Two is where their stories move from creation to connection, from readiness to rollout, and from kitchen to consumer.

In the chapters ahead, you'll see how each founder approaches placement and promotion through the lens of their brand stage, budget, and capacity. Some will move cautiously, others more aggressively, but each will confront the same industry truths, that distribution requires discipline, promotion demands planning, and visibility must be earned and sustained. Their journeys reveal how strategic decisions made at this stage can either support momentum or quietly undermine it.

As their brands gain traction, a new set of challenges begins to surface. Growth introduces complexity, more partners, more moving parts, and more decisions that can no longer be made on instinct alone. These realities set the stage for Book Three, where the focus shifts from being in the market to building an organization that can support it. There, you'll follow the founders as they learn to assemble the right people, define roles, establish systems, and translate their experiences into a structured business plan designed for long-term success.

CHAPTER ONE

Placement (Distribution)

When I began working in the industry in 2006, I quickly realized that distribution was one of the least understood aspects of launching a food product. That shroud of mystery remains, as many founders still assume that once they have their product in a few stores, everything else will "just work." But in CPG, how your product moves is just as important as how it tastes or looks.

Distribution is where logistics meets relationships. It's the network that connects your manufacturing, warehousing, retailers, and ultimately your consumers. It affects your pricing, profitability, freshness, and brand reputation, often more than any marketing campaign ever could.

I've spent years navigating this space: negotiating with distributors, exploring DSD networks, working alongside logistics teams, and troubleshooting last-minute shipping issues the week before a national sales campaign. And here's what I've learned, smart distribution is about strategy and having the right partners, the right channels, and the right systems to ensure that your product is where it's supposed to be when it's supposed to be there .

In this chapter, I'll help you understand the supply chain from end to end, demystify the terminology, and show you how to select distribution models that match your product's needs and your business goals. Because the truth is, poor distribution can kill a great brand, but great distribution can turn a small one into a household name.

Supply Chain Overview

Before diving into distributors, brokers, and retailers, it's important to step back and understand the big picture of the food supply chain. For a packaged food startup, the supply chain is the network of steps and partners that move your product from concept to consumer. Every handoff impacts cost, timing, and ultimately your ability to succeed at retail.

Think of the supply chain as the highway system that carries your brand. If you don't understand how the lanes connect, you risk traffic jams, detours, or dead ends that eat away at profits.

The Flow of Goods in Food

Every food product begins with raw materials and ingredients. This is where the supply chain truly starts, with farmers, ingredient suppliers, and processors providing the core components that go into your product. This stage also includes packaging suppliers, such as those producing labels, cartons, jars, bottles, and other materials that protect, preserve, and present your product for sale.

Next comes manufacturing or co-packing, where raw ingredients are transformed into finished goods. Depending on the stage of your business, this may happen in your own production facility, a shared-use commercial kitchen, or through a third-party co-packer. This phase is where recipes are standardized, food safety protocols are enforced, and products are prepared at scale for distribution.

Once manufactured, finished goods move into a warehouse or third-party logistics provider, commonly referred to as a 3PL. These facilities store inventory until orders are placed and may also handle pick, pack, and ship functions. For many early-stage brands, 3PLs play a critical role in managing inventory efficiently without the need to invest in owned warehousing.

From there, products enter the distribution layer. Distributors either purchase your product outright or manage it on consignment, storing it in their own facilities and delivering it to retailers or food-service accounts. This layer includes national distributors such as UNFI and KeHE, regional distributors, and direct-store-delivery operators, each serving different channels and geographies.

The next stop is the retailer or foodservice account. Grocery chains, independent retailers, club stores, and restaurants are the points where your product finally meets the consumer. At this stage, shelf placement, pricing, and in-store support all influence whether a shopper notices, tries, and repurchases your product.

Finally, the flow ends with the consumer, the person who buys, eats, and hopefully comes back for more. Every decision made earlier in the supply chain ultimately impacts this moment, making it essential for founders to understand how each layer affects product quality, availability, and the overall customer experience.

The Flow of Goods in Food

Raw Materials and Ingredients

- Where it all starts: farmers, ingredient suppliers, and processors.

- Includes packaging suppliers (labels, boxes, bottles, etc.).

Manufacturing / Co-Packing

- Where your ingredients are transformed into finished product.

- May include your own facility, a shared-use kitchen, or a co-packer.

Warehouse / 3PL (Third-Party Logistics)

- Finished goods are stored until orders are received.

- 3PL partners can also handle pick, pack, and ship functions.

Distribution Layer

- Distributors purchase your product (or manage it on consignment), store it, and deliver it to retailers or foodservice accounts.

- Includes large nationals (UNFI, KeHE), regionals, and direct-store-delivery (DSD) operators.

Retailer or Foodservice Account

- The grocery chains, independents, club stores, or restaurants that put your product in front of consumers.

Consumer

- The end customer who buys, eats, and (hopefully) comes back for more.

Figure: The Flow of Goods in Food

Why Founders Must
Understand the Supply Chain

For food founders, understanding the supply chain is essential to maintaining control over costs. Every step in the journey, from sourcing ingredients to delivering finished goods, adds expense. When founders know where money is being spent and why, they are better equipped to protect margins, make informed trade-offs, and avoid surprises that erode profitability.

Supply chain knowledge also drives efficiency. Clear visibility into lead times, freight requirements, and delivery schedules helps prevent stockouts, late shipments, and costly penalties. When founders understand how long each step takes and who is responsible at every stage, they can plan inventory and production more accurately, reducing stress and operational disruption.

Scalability is another critical reason to understand how the supply chain works. The systems that support selling a few hundred cases are rarely the same ones that can handle tens of thousands. Planning for growth early allows founders to transition smoothly as volume increases, rather than scrambling to rebuild processes under pressure.

Finally, supply chain fluency is a core component of retail readiness. Buyers expect founders to clearly explain how their product will move from production to shelf, including storage, distribution, and delivery. Demonstrating this understanding builds credibility and signals that the brand is prepared to operate at retail standards, not just produce a great product.

Simplified Example: Granola Bar Supply Chain

Ingredients (oats, chocolate, nuts) →

Co-Packer produces cases of bars →

Shipped to a 3PL warehouse →

Sold to UNFI distributor →

Delivered to Whole Foods DC (distribution center) →

Stocked in stores →

Shopper buys off shelf

At each handoff, costs (freight, storage, margins) are added. By the time your $1.00 bar leaves your co-packer, it may pass through 3–4 partners before reaching a consumer at $2.99–$3.49 retail.

Figure: Granola Bar Supply Chain Simplified Example

How Supply Chain Decisions Affect Everything Else

Your supply chain decisions have downstream effects across every area of your business. Ingredient sourcing influences product quality, cost structure, and the credibility of any sustainability claims you make. Co-packer selection affects consistency, scalability, and adherence to food safety standards, all of which are critical as you grow. Logistics decisions determine how quickly your product reaches the market and what you spend on transportation. Packaging choices impact freight efficiency, shelf life, and how your product is perceived by consumers. Inventory management plays a direct role in cash flow and storage costs, while data tracking supports traceability, regulatory compliance, and the level of trust you build with retail partners. Each link in the chain either reinforces or weakens the next. Strong systems and reliable partners create flow, while weak links introduce friction that can slow or disrupt your growth.

How Supply Chain Decisions Affect Everything Else

Your supply chain decisions have downstream effects across every area of your business:

Decision Area	Impact
Ingredient sourcing	Affects quality, cost, and sustainability claims
Co-packer selection	Influences consistency, scalability, and food safety
Logistics	Determines speed to market and shipping costs
Packaging	Impacts freight efficiency, shelf life, and consumer appeal
Inventory management	Affects cash flow and storage costs
Data tracking	Supports traceability, compliance, and retailer trust

Each link reinforces or weakens the next. Strong systems and reliable partners create flow; weak links create friction.

How Supply Chain Decisions Affect Everything Else

BONUS - SUPPLY CHAIN VS. VALUE CHAIN

Many use the terms *supply chain* and *value chain* interchangeably in food CPG, but they describe two distinct concepts. Understanding the difference helps founders think more clearly about operations, economics, and long-term impact.

The supply chain refers to the system and resources required to move a product from supplier to customer. It focuses on *flow and execution*: sourcing raw materials and packaging, manufacturing or co-packing, warehousing, transportation, distribution, and delivery to retail or foodservice accounts. When founders are thinking about lead times, freight costs, cold chain requirements, minimum order quantities, or distributor logistics, they are dealing with the supply chain. In simple terms, the supply chain answers the question: *How does the product physically move from origin to shelf, and what systems are required to make that happen?*

The value chain builds on the supply chain by examining *how value is added at each stage of that journey*, both to the product itself and to the actors involved. In manufacturing and business terms, the value chain includes all activities through which a company creates value, including production, marketing, sales, distribution, and after-sales service. It looks not only at movement, but at transformation: how ingredients become a finished product, how packaging, branding, pricing, and positioning enhance perceived value, and how customer support, feedback, and service extend value beyond the initial purchase.

From a broader perspective, the value chain also encourages a full-lifecycle view. Rather than focusing only on upstream inputs, it considers what happens before, during, and after the sale. This includes how value is distributed across internal teams, external partners, retailers, and consumers, and how decisions affect long-term viability. While value is often measured in economic terms, it can also encompass non-monetary dimensions such as ethical sourcing, labor practices, environmental stewardship, waste reduction, and added customer utility.

For founders, the distinction matters because a product can move efficiently through a supply chain without creating lasting value, and a strong value proposition can fail if the underlying supply chain cannot support it. Sustainable food businesses are built when both are aligned: when operational execution supports value creation, and when value creation is grounded in operational reality. Thinking in terms of both chains helps founders design businesses that function well, scale responsibly, and create value not just at the shelf, but across the entire system.

Channel Strategy

Not every product belongs in every channel, at least not right away. A channel strategy is your roadmap for deciding *where* and *how* to sell your product based on your resources, category, and long-term goals. Picking the right first channel can make or break your brand's launch, while an undisciplined approach can stretch you thin and burn cash.

What Is a Channel?

A channel is simply the path your product takes to reach the consumer. Each one comes with its own expectations, economics, and role in your brand's growth journey.

Common Food Channels:

- **Grocery and Supermarkets** – Conventional retailers like Kroger, Safeway, or regional chains.

- **Natural/Specialty Stores** – Whole Foods, Sprouts, co-ops, or gourmet markets.

- **Mass Retailers** – Walmart, Target, and club stores like Costco or Sam's Club.

- **Convenience (C-Store)** – 7-Eleven, gas stations, travel hubs.

- **E-commerce/DTC** – Shopify, Amazon, Thrive Market, or your own website.

- **Foodservice** – Schools, universities, restaurants, corporate dining, airlines.

- **Alternative Channels** – Subscription boxes, gyms, gift shops, military commissaries.

Why Channel Strategy Matters

Choosing the right channel is one of the most consequential decisions a food founder will make, because not every product belongs everywhere. Pack size, price point, and usage occasion often determine whether a product is better suited for club, convenience, natural, specialty, or conventional grocery. Channel selection also has a direct impact on your financial model, as slotting fees, distributor margins, promotional expectations, and trade spend vary widely and can dramatically alter profitability. Beyond economics, channel choice shapes brand perception. A launch at Erewhon communicates something very different to consumers than a debut at Walmart, even if the product itself is the same.

Finally, channel strategy is as much about timing as it is about fit. The most successful brands rarely attempt to launch everywhere at once. Instead, they build traction and operational confidence in one channel, then expand deliberately, using early wins to support smarter, more sustainable growth.

Building a Channel Strategy

An effective channel strategy starts with a clear understanding of your consumer. Founders need to ask where their target customer already shops and what they are seeking in that environment, whether it's a premium experience, everyday convenience, or strong value. Channel decisions should then align closely with the product itself. Shelf-stable snacks often perform well in grocery, convenience, and e-commerce, while frozen meals require the infrastructure of grocery, club, or select specialty retailers. Beverages frequently succeed in convenience, grocery, and foodservice, where impulse and repeat purchase drive volume.

Just as important is choosing where you can realistically win first. For many early-stage brands, regional natural grocers or a direct-to-consumer model provide more accessible entry points than national mass retail, which carries higher costs and operational demands. Successful founders think in phases, not leaps. Initial traction may come from local natural retailers and DTC, followed by regional grocery and scaled e-commerce, and only later expansion into national grocery, mass, or club once systems, capital, and velocity can support it.

As you expand, channel conflict must be managed intentionally. Pricing should remain consistent across channels to protect brand credibility and retailer relationships, while pack sizes and formats can be tailored to different environments to avoid direct comparisons. Thoughtful channel sequencing allows brands to grow with control, protect margins, and maintain a cohesive brand story as they scale.

Real-World Simulation

A premium kombucha brand launched exclusively in natural retailers (Whole Foods, co-ops) to build credibility and prove velocity. Once it gained traction, it expanded into regional grocery (Safeway, Kroger divisions). Years later, it launched into club stores with larger packs and into convenience for on-the-go formats. By sequencing strategically, the brand avoided overextending early and preserved its premium positioning while scaling.

Pro Tip: Your channel strategy should be as much about saying *no* as it is about saying *yes*. Focus on the channels that reinforce your brand positioning and can realistically support your operations. Expansion comes with time, data, and a strong foundation.

Distribution Options

How your product reaches the shelf is just as important as the product itself. Distribution is not a one-size-fits-all decision; it is a strategic choice that influences your margins, your control over the business, your speed to market, and your long-term scalability. Founders are often presented with two primary paths early on: selling direct to retailers or working through distributors. Each approach comes with distinct advantages, trade-offs, and operational requirements.

Selling direct offers greater control and higher margins, allowing you to build relationships with retailers, manage pricing more closely, and maintain visibility into orders and performance. It is often the preferred path in early stages or within local and regional markets. However, it also requires more hands-on management, from logistics to invoicing, and can limit how quickly you scale.

Working with distributors introduces reach and efficiency. Distributors provide access to established retail networks, consolidated logistics, and operational infrastructure that would be difficult to replicate independently. At the same time, this model introduces additional costs, reduced margin, and less direct control over how your product moves through the system.

The sections that follow explore each option in detail, helping you understand when to leverage one over the other, and how to structure your approach based on your stage of growth, resources, and long-term objectives.

SELLING DIRECT

Selling direct is often the first retail entry point for emerging food brands. Instead of starting with a distributor or broker, founders approach stores themselves, building early shelf presence while avoiding the complexity and cost of large-scale distribution. This approach allows brands to test their product in real retail environments, learn how buyers respond, and generate early sales data before committing to broader expansion.

Local independent grocers are typically the most accessible starting point. These retailers value differentiation and often seek out local or emerging brands that resonate with their customer base. Founders usually contact the store's buyer or category manager directly, provide samples and a concise sell sheet outlining pricing, case size, and delivery terms, and manage the relationship themselves. In many cases, delivery is handled by the founder in a direct-store-delivery style until volume justifies working with a distributor. Strong relationships matter here. When store managers and staff genuinely like a product, they often become informal advocates, recommending it to shoppers and helping it gain traction.

Some national retailers also offer local or regional vendor programs designed to spotlight small or emerging brands. Chains like Walmart, Kroger, and Whole Foods use these programs to introduce unique products without requiring immediate national scale. The process typically involves an online application and basic operational readiness, such as business licenses, insurance, UPCs, and EDI capability. Approved products may launch in a limited number of stores or a regional cluster, with the opportunity to expand if performance is strong. These programs should be viewed as proving grounds. Consistent sell-through, reliable supply, and operational discipline are what turn a local test into broader placement.

The benefits of selling direct are significant. It provides proof of concept through real sales data, keeps founders close to customers, and lowers the barriers to entry compared to distributor-led expansion. It also offers flexibility, allowing brands to refine pricing, packaging, and merchandising before scaling production. At the same time, this path comes with challenges. Direct selling is time-intensive, logistics and invoicing fall on the founder, reach is limited compared to distributor networks, and cash flow can be tight with Net 30 or longer payment terms. For many founders, selling direct is not the end goal, but a strategic first step that builds credibility, insight, and momentum for what comes next.

Pro Tip: Selling direct is often a rite of passage for food entrepreneurs. Embrace it as a chance to learn, build relationships, and prove your brand in the marketplace. If your product can move off the shelf without national marketing support, you'll be well-positioned to scale into larger retail opportunities.

DISTRIBUTORS

Once you've proven demand through direct selling or local vendor programs, scaling usually requires working with a distributor. Distributors act as the middle link between you and the retailer, buying your product, warehousing it, and delivering it to stores on their routes.

Not all distributors are the same. They differ in the retailers they serve, the categories they specialize in, and the expectations they have of suppliers. Founders need to understand these differences to pick the right partners and plan their sales strategy.

Natural Distributors

(Ex. UNFI, KeHE)

Overview:

- These are the most prominent natural/organic distributors in North America, serving retailers like Whole Foods, Sprouts, Natural Grocers, and co-ops.

- They are often the *first stop* for better-for-you, specialty, or niche products looking to scale regionally and nationally.

Why They Matter:

- They provide access to thousands of accounts across natural, specialty, and conventional channels.

- Retailers like Whole Foods often require new brands to be carried through UNFI or KeHE.

Considerations:

- **Costly:** Distributor fees, chargebacks, and promotional expectations can be high.

- **Picky:** They prefer brands that already have retail demand or retailer authorization.

- **Slow to Onboard:** It can take months from first contact to being in their system.

. . .

Pro Tip: Don't pitch UNFI or KeHE too early. Most brands need existing retail demand (buyers requesting product) before being taken on.

Mainline Distributors

(Ex. Performance Food Group, US Foods, C&S)

Overview:

- Large distributors serving broad categories of retailers and foodservice operators.

- Often supply conventional grocery chains, independent supermarkets, and institutional accounts.

Why They Matter:

- Scale and efficiency, these distributors move massive volumes of food across the U.S.

- Useful for brands transitioning from regional independents to mid-size grocery chains.

- They often serve foodservice, which can open institutional opportunities (schools, hospitals, corporate dining).

Considerations:

- They prioritize established brands that can move volume.

- Fees and slotting at distribution centers are common.

- Less likely to nurture early-stage startups compared to natural distributors.

Pro Tip: Mainline distributors are powerful once your brand has traction, but they are rarely the right entry point for first-time founders.

Channel-Specific Distributors

(Ex. Core-Mark, McLane, H.T. Hackney, SpartanNash)

Overview:

- These distributors specialize in specific retail channels, most notably convenience stores, drugstores, and regional supermarkets.

- Core-Mark and McLane, for example, dominate the U.S. convenience store distribution system.

Why They Matter:

- They control access to thousands of small-format stores nationwide.

- Perfect for on-the-go products like snacks, beverages, and impulse buys.

- Essential for brands that want to penetrate C-store, drug, or military channels.

Considerations:

- High expectations for velocity, slow movers get cut quickly.

- Limited marketing support compared to natural distributors.

- Regional coverage varies, not all distributors cover the entire U.S.

Pro Tip: Use channel-specific distributors after you know your product performs well in that channel. For example, test in a few convenience stores before pitching Core-Mark nationally.

Key Takeaway

Don't chase *all* distributors at once. Pick the one that best matches your channel strategy and build a strong relationship. Distributors are long-term partners, and breaking into their systems requires commitment, trade spend, and consistent execution.

It's imperative to align with the right distributor for your product, category, and growth stage. Natural distributors open the door to health-focused retailers, mainline distributors bring scale, and channel-specific distributors unlock niche but powerful channels like convenience and drug.

Logistics Overview

Once your product is made, it has to get from your facility (or co-packer) to the retailer, distributor, or direct consumer. This is where logistics comes in. Logistics covers the storage, handling, and movement of your product. For food founders, it's often one of the least glamorous parts of the business, but it can make or break your ability to deliver reliably, protect margins, and scale smoothly.

Most startups face a big decision early: Should we manage logistics ourselves or outsource it to a third-party logistics provider (3PL)? The right choice depends on your resources, volume, and channel mix.

3PL (Third-Party Logistics)

A third-party logistics provider, or 3PL, is a company that stores your finished products and manages order fulfillment on your behalf. After production, you ship goods to the 3PL's warehouse, where inventory is stored until orders are received from distributors, retailers, or direct-to-consumer channels. Once an order comes in, the 3PL handles picking, packing, and shipping according to your specifications. In exchange, you pay for storage, handling, and freight-related services.

For many founders, the primary advantage of a 3PL is flexibility. These partners are built to scale, making it easier to grow volume without investing in your own warehouse or staff. They also bring operational expertise, including familiarity with retailer compliance requirements, labeling standards, routing guides, and delivery windows. Many 3PLs operate multiple facilities across regions, which can shorten shipping times and improve service levels. Most importantly, outsourcing logistics allows founders to focus on sales, marketing, and brand-building rather than running a warehouse.

At the same time, working with a 3PL requires thoughtful oversight. Fees can accumulate quickly through storage, pick-and-pack, and minimum volume charges. Once inventory leaves your facility, you also give up some direct control, making clear SOPs, reporting, and communication critical. System integration matters as well— your 3PL must work seamlessly with your e-commerce platform, distributors, and accounting tools to avoid costly errors.

Pros

- Scales easily as order volume grows

- Reduces upfront capital investment in warehousing and labor

- Provides retail-compliant logistics expertise

- Frees founders to focus on growth-driving activities

Cons

- Ongoing fees can impact margins if not monitored closely

- Less hands-on control over inventory handling

- Technology and system integration can be complex

- Minimums and contracts may limit flexibility

Pro Tip: For most early-stage food brands, a 3PL offers the best balance between professionalism and practicality, providing the infrastructure retailers expect without the cost and complexity of building it yourself.

Owned logistics

Owned logistics means managing your fulfillment and distribution operations entirely in-house, using your own warehouse space, staff, and transportation resources (or leased vehicles). Instead of outsourcing storage and shipping, your company is responsible for every operational step once the product leaves manufacturing.

In this model, you lease or own warehouse space and build an internal team to receive inventory, store it, pick and pack orders, and prepare shipments. You also manage freight relationships directly, negotiating rates with carriers and ensuring deliveries meet retailer routing guides and delivery requirements. This approach gives founders end-to-end control, but it also places the full operational burden on the business.

The primary benefit of owned logistics is control. You have full visibility into inventory levels, handling procedures, shipping schedules, and quality standards. This can be especially valuable for brands with highly customized packing needs, complex kitting, or sensitive products. At very large volumes, owned logistics can also become more cost-effective than paying per-unit 3PL fees, as fixed costs are spread across higher throughput.

However, owned logistics introduces significant complexity and financial risk. Warehousing infrastructure, equipment, software, insurance, and labor create high fixed overhead. Compliance responsibilities, from food safety protocols to retailer routing guides, become your responsibility. Most importantly, logistics management can quickly consume time and energy that would otherwise be spent on sales, marketing, and product innovation.

Pros

- Full control over inventory handling and fulfillment
- Greater flexibility for custom packing, kitting, or DTC experiences
- Potential cost efficiencies at very high volumes
- Direct oversight of service levels and quality

Cons

- High upfront and ongoing capital costs
- Operational complexity and compliance burden
- Requires dedicated management and specialized expertise
- Can distract founders from growth-driving priorities

Owned logistics is rarely the right choice for early-stage food brands. It typically becomes viable only at meaningful scale, often $20M+ in annual revenue, or when products require specialized handling that most 3PLs cannot support efficiently.

Direct Store Delivery (DSD)

Direct Store Delivery (DSD) is a logistics and distribution model in which the manufacturer delivers products directly to individual retail stores, bypassing the retailer's distribution center entirely. In this model, the vendor is responsible not only for delivery, but often for in-store execution, including stocking shelves, rotating inventory, and setting up displays. DSD gives brands a high degree of control over how their products appear and perform at shelf.

With DSD, the manufacturer or an independent route operator owns or leases the delivery vehicles and services a defined set of stores on a regular schedule. Drivers frequently function as merchandisers, checking inventory levels, maintaining shelf facings, rotating product by date, and building approved displays. Retailers favor this model in certain categories because it reduces store labor, ensures fresher product, and maintains consistent on-shelf availability.

DSD is most common in categories where freshness, speed, and frequent replenishment are critical. Beverages rely on DSD to keep high-volume SKUs constantly stocked and cold. Salty snacks use DSD to support heavy promotional calendars and secure prime shelf real estate. Bread and baked goods depend on DSD to manage short shelf lives and rapid turnover. In these categories, large manufacturers often act as category captains, using their DSD infrastructure to influence shelf sets, promotions, and resets.

Pros

- Direct control over delivery, stocking, and merchandising
- Fresher product and faster replenishment cycles
- Stronger shelf presence through maintained facings and displays
- Reduced reliance on retailer labor

Cons

- Capital-intensive (trucks, fuel, drivers, insurance)
- Operationally complex to manage routes and labor
- Difficult to scale beyond limited geographies without major investment
- Rarely feasible for small or emerging brands

The DSD Reality for Startups

While DSD sounds appealing, getting your product directly into stores without going through a distributor's warehouse, the reality is:

- **High Barriers to Entry:** Trucks, drivers, merchandising staff, and fuel costs make it extremely expensive.

- **Retailer Resistance:** Most chains reserve DSD access for their biggest vendors and category captains.

- **Independent Routes:** Smaller DSD opportunities exist via independent route owners (franchise-style) who deliver certain products, but they generally focus on established, high-velocity categories.

- **Limited Exceptions:** Some major chains (like Kroger or Walmart) may allow small vendors to operate "local vendor programs," where you deliver product directly to a handful of stores. But this rarely scales beyond a small regional footprint.

Figure: The DSD Reality for Startups

DSD is powerful but expensive. For most startup food brands, it's not realistic at launch. It becomes viable only in very specific categories or at scale, when volume, margins, and retailer expectations can justify the operational investment.

Pro Tip: Don't confuse *local store delivery* (you dropping off cases at a few stores) with true DSD. For almost all startups, DSD is not a scalable strategy. Focus instead on distributor-based models unless your category and funding truly justify otherwise.

SPEAKING LOGISTICS

For many founders, the logistics can feel intimidating. The world of logistics comes with its own language, and it can feel like alphabet soup. On top of that, many retailers, distributors, and 3PLs expect you to understand their terminology, and miscommunication can be costly.

It's important to familiarize yourself with logistics terms for a better understanding of how product moves, what you're paying for, and how to hold partners accountable.

Accessorial Charges

Extra fees charged by carriers for services beyond standard delivery. Common examples include liftgate service, inside delivery, detention/wait time, appointment scheduling, or residential delivery. These charges can add up quickly and often appear after delivery, so invoices should always be reviewed carefully.

Bill of Lading (BOL)

A legal document issued by the carrier that details what is being shipped, where it's going, and under what terms. It serves as the official receipt for freight.

It confirms what the shipper hands over, protects both shipper and carrier in the event of damage or shortages, and is often required for invoicing and freight claims.

Carrier

The company physically transporting the freight. This can be a trucking company, rail operator, ocean carrier, or airline. Carriers are responsible for moving goods according to the terms outlined in the Bill of Lading.

Cold Chain

A temperature-controlled supply chain required for refrigerated or frozen products. From manufacturing to storage to transportation, specific temperature ranges must be maintained to ensure food safety, quality, and regulatory compliance.

Consolidation

The process of combining multiple smaller shipments into one larger shipment to reduce freight costs. Consolidation is often managed by 3PLs or freight forwarders and is commonly used with LTL shipments.

Consignee

The company receiving the goods. This may be a distributor, retailer, warehouse, or direct customer. The consignee is listed on shipping documents and often signs the Proof of Delivery.

Cross Docking

A logistics practice where product is unloaded from one truck and immediately reloaded onto another with little or no storage in between. This speeds up delivery and reduces warehousing costs but requires precise coordination and scheduling.

Distribution Center (DC)

A warehouse where products are received, stored, and redistributed to retail stores or other destinations. Large retailers such as Walmart, Kroger, and Costco operate their own DCs, and suppliers must ship into these facilities following strict routing guidelines.

Distributor

A company that buys your product, stores it, and resells it to retailers or foodservice accounts. Distributors typically add a margin of 15–25% to your wholesale price and play a key role in scaling distribution.

ETA (Estimated Time of Arrival)

The expected delivery time of a shipment. Accurate ETAs are critical for warehouse staffing, retailer appointments, inventory planning, and avoiding late-delivery penalties.

Fill Rate

A measure of how much of an order is fulfilled. If a retailer orders 100 cases and you ship 90, your fill rate is 90%. Consistently low fill rates can frustrate buyers and jeopardize shelf space.

First In, First Out (FIFO)

An inventory management method where the oldest stock is shipped or sold first. FIFO is essential in food and beverage to maintain freshness and prevent expired product.

Freight

A general term for goods being transported in bulk for commercial purposes. Freight typically moves via truck, rail, ocean, or air and differs from small-parcel shipping such as UPS or FedEx.

Freight Forwarder

A company that organizes shipments on your behalf. Freight forwarders do not physically move the goods but arrange carriers, manage documentation, and handle customs clearance, particularly for international shipments.

Full Truckload (FTL)

A shipment that fills an entire truck, usually 24–26 pallets or 40,000+ pounds.

FTL offers lower cost per unit, faster transit, and less handling, but it can be expensive if you don't have enough volume to fill the truck.

Inbound Logistics

The movement of goods into your business. This includes ingredients, packaging, and supplies delivered to your facility or co-packer.

Intermodal

A shipment that uses multiple modes of transportation (such as truck to rail to truck) under a single contract. Intermodal shipping is often more cost-effective and sustainable but may take longer.

Just In Time (JIT)

An inventory strategy where goods arrive just as they are needed for production or sale. JIT reduces storage costs but increases risk if there are delays or supply chain disruptions.

Landed Cost

The total cost of getting your product to its final destination. This includes ingredients, packaging, labor, freight, duties, and fees. Understanding landed cost is critical for accurate pricing and margin planning.

Lead Time

The time between when an order is placed and when it is delivered. Retailers and distributors expect reliable lead times, and missing them can result in penalties or lost trust.

Less Than Truckload (LTL)

A shipment that does not fill an entire truck and is combined with other shippers' freight.

LTL is more affordable for smaller shipments but involves more handling, increasing the risk of delays or damage.

Outbound Logistics

The movement of finished goods out of your business. This includes shipments to distributors, retailers, foodservice accounts, or direct-to-consumer customers.

Packing List

A document that lists all items included in a shipment. It travels with the freight and is used by the consignee to verify contents upon delivery.

Pallet

A wooden or plastic platform, typically 40x48 inches in the U.S., used to stack and move cases of product. Most retailers require standardized pallets to fit their material handling systems.

Pick and Pack

The process of selecting products from inventory ("picking") and packing them into boxes for shipment. This is especially common in e-commerce and DTC fulfillment.

Proof of Delivery (POD)

A signed document, often electronic, confirming that goods were delivered in full and in acceptable condition. PODs are frequently required by retailers and distributors before payment is released.

Shipper

The company sending the goods. In most cases, this is the manufacturer or brand owner listed on the Bill of Lading.

Distribution Strategies by Channel

Not every channel is right for every product, and successful brands rarely launch everywhere at once. Each channel comes with its own expectations, economics, and operational demands. Understanding how these channels differ allows founders to sequence their growth realistically, align distribution with their resources, and avoid costly missteps that can derail an otherwise strong product.

Conventional Grocery

Conventional grocery includes national and regional supermarket chains such as Kroger, Safeway, Publix, and their regional counterparts. For many founders, grocery feels like the ultimate destination because of its scale and visibility, but it is also one of the most competitive and expensive channels to enter. The most effective approach is typically to start regionally with one or two banners rather than attempting a national rollout. Data from smaller channels can help demonstrate velocity and consumer demand before expanding. Grocery retailers expect consistent promotions, slotting fees, and ongoing trade support, so budgeting for these requirements is essential.

. . .

Specialty Retail

Specialty retailers, including gourmet markets, food halls, and high-end independents, are often ideal for premium products, unique imports, or brands with a compelling story. While overall volume is lower than conventional grocery, margins are often higher and the credibility gained can be meaningful. Many brands use specialty as a launchpad before scaling into larger channels. Relationships play an outsized role here, and founder-led tastings or in-store storytelling can significantly influence buyer and shopper engagement.

Natural and Organic

Natural and organic-focused retailers such as Whole Foods, Sprouts, Natural Grocers, and independent natural markets are a strong entry point for clean-label, better-for-you products. These retailers are often more open to emerging brands than conventional grocery, though they maintain strict standards around ingredients, sourcing, and sustainability claims. Programs like Whole Foods' local forager initiatives can help early-stage brands gain entry without immediate national distribution, making this channel a common first step for many founders.

Mass Merchandisers

Mass retailers like Walmart and Target offer enormous volume potential, but they operate on thin margins and require substantial trade spend and operational readiness. Brands should consider mass only after proving velocity and execution in smaller channels. The ability to scale quickly, maintain fill rates, and support sudden volume spikes is critical. Entering mass too early can strain supply chains and damage brand credibility if execution falls short.

. . .

Drug

Drugstore chains such as CVS, Walgreens, and Rite Aid are well suited for on-the-go products, including snacks, beverages, and functional foods. These stores can be effective for building trial and convenience-driven awareness, often through checkout or high-traffic aisles. Distribution is frequently managed through partners like McLane, and strong packaging is critical, as many purchases are impulsive and driven by visual appeal.

Club

Warehouse clubs like Costco, Sam's Club, and BJ's are built around high-volume sales and bulk pack sizes. This channel works best for established products with strong trial and repeat purchase. Club typically requires unique SKUs and packaging formats, and large purchase orders can create cash flow volatility. Founders must be prepared to finance big production runs and manage delayed payments before committing to this channel.

Convenience

Convenience stores, including gas stations, travel plazas, and small-format chains, thrive on impulse purchases and single-serve items. Velocity is paramount, as slow-moving products are quickly discontinued. Distribution often relies on DSD models or large distributors such as Core-Mark or McLane. Many brands benefit from testing in regional chains before pursuing national convenience rollouts.

Co-ops

Consumer-owned co-ops are a natural fit for mission-driven, local, or natural brands. These stores are typically more flexible in onboarding new products and supportive of small businesses. While volumes are modest, co-ops offer strong credibility with values-driven shoppers who are often eager to provide feedback. This channel can overlap nicely with DTC efforts and early-stage validation.

Military

Military commissaries and exchanges serve a nationwide network of loyal shoppers and are managed through the Defense Commissary Agency. While the procurement process is slow and requires specific approvals, this channel can be a powerful niche opportunity for categories like snacks, beverages, and shelf-stable staples. Persistence and relationship-building are essential, but growth tends to be steady once established.

Travel Retail

Travel retail includes airports, train stations, cruise ships, and duty-free environments. These outlets favor premium, portable, and giftable products that stand out in limited shelf space. Partnerships with concession operators are often required, and while volumes can vary, the visibility and brand exposure can be significant. Packaging must be eye-catching and justify premium pricing.

Foodservice

Foodservice and institutional channels encompass restaurants, universities, hospitals, corporate dining, and stadiums, typically accessed through broadline distributors such as Sysco or US Foods. These channels are well suited for bulk-pack products or ingredients and can provide consistent volume with lower marketing spend. However, sales cycles are longer, and products are often used behind the scenes, limiting direct brand visibility with consumers.

E-commerce

E-commerce, including direct-to-consumer platforms like Shopify and marketplaces such as Amazon or Thrive Market, is often a starting point for early validation and brand building. This channel offers a direct feedback loop with customers and flexibility to test SKUs, pricing, and messaging. At the same time, shipping, fulfillment, and digital marketing costs can be high, so founders should use e-commerce strategically as a learning and testing tool rather than assuming it will be instantly profitable.

Pro Tip: Don't try to enter all channels at once. Pick 1–2 that align best with your product and resources, win there, then expand strategically.

Sourcing Platforms

In today's food industry, many buyers don't just wait for trade shows or distributor reps to introduce them to new products, they actively use digital sourcing platforms. These platforms connect brands with retailers, distributors, and other buyers who are searching for emerging products to bring into their assortments.

For founders, being on these platforms is about visibility and accessibility. Buyers may not discover you otherwise, but on these platforms they can view your profile, request samples, and even place orders directly.

Why They're Important

- **Discovery:** Platforms are often the first stop for buyers searching for new products in a category.

- **Accessibility:** Buyers can find you 24/7, without waiting for a trade show.

- **Validation:** Many large retailers now *require* brand profiles on certain platforms (ex., RangeMe).

- **Efficiency:** They streamline the process of sharing product details, certifications, pricing, and case packs.

KEY PLATFORMS

RangeMe

Overview:

- The most widely recognized product discovery platform, especially for large retailers.

- Used by giants like Target, Kroger, CVS, and Walmart to source new brands.

- Brands upload product info, certifications, pricing, and samples for buyers to review.

Why It's Important:

- Many retailers require a RangeMe profile even to be considered for review.

- It standardizes submissions, so buyers can quickly compare products.

- Premium (paid) tiers increase visibility by placing your profile in front of more buyers.

How to List:

- Create a free profile with product photos, case pack, pricing, certifications (organic, non-GMO, etc.).

- Invest in strong imagery and concise copy, buyers scan dozens of profiles at once.

- Consider Premium for faster access, but even free profiles get visibility if optimized.

Pro Tip: Treat your RangeMe profile like a mini website. Many buyers make snap judgments based on how professional it looks.

Mable

Overview:

- A wholesale ordering platform designed to connect emerging brands with independent retailers and small chains.

- Think of it as a modern wholesale marketplace with simplified ordering, no giant distributor in the middle.

Why It's Important:

- Great for scaling regionally, especially if you're not yet ready for UNFI or KeHE.

- Independent retailers trust Mable as a curated source for new and local products.

- Provides fulfillment flexibility, brands can ship DTC to stores, or use Mable fulfillment support.

How to List:

- Create a brand storefront with product photos, wholesale pricing, and order minimums.

- Offer incentives like free shipping or first-order discounts to attract early buyers.

- Keep inventory updated, independent retailers value reliability.

Pro Tip: Mable is particularly useful for natural, specialty, and local brands targeting the independent retail channel.

Faire

Overview:

- Originally a marketplace for independent boutiques and lifestyle retailers, now expanded into food and beverage.

- Popular among specialty shops, cafes, and gift retailers.

- Known for flexible terms like net 60 and free returns on first orders.

Why It's Important:

- Great for getting into non-traditional retail outlets like coffee shops, gift stores, and lifestyle retailers that carry grab-and-go foods.

- High discoverability, stores search by category, location, or trending products.

- Provides built-in risk reduction for buyers, making them more likely to test new brands.

How to List:

- Set up a storefront with high-quality imagery, detailed descriptions, and wholesale case pricing.

- Take advantage of Faire promotions (free shipping, first-order discounts) to encourage trial.

- Track performance via Faire analytics to see which SKUs and regions are gaining traction.

Pro Tip: Faire is best for premium, giftable, or impulse foods rather than pantry staples. It's especially strong if your packaging has a "lifestyle" or "design-forward" appeal.

How They Differ

Platform	Best For	Buyer Audience	Key Advantage	Typical Use Case
RangeMe	Retail readiness	Large national and regional retailers	Standardized submissions	Required for category reviews (ex., Target, CVS)
Mable	Early-stage wholesale	Independent retailers, small chains	Easy wholesale onboarding	Regional growth, natural/specialty stores
Faire	Lifestyle and specialty crossover	Boutiques, cafes, gift shops	Buyer-friendly terms (net 60, free returns)	Expanding beyond grocery into lifestyle retail

Table: How The Platforms Differ

Pro Tip: Many successful founders use all three platforms strategically: RangeMe to access major retailers, Mable to build regional momentum with independents, and Faire to tap into non-traditional channels.

HOW TO OPTIMIZE YOUR SOURCING PLATFORM PROFILE

Your profile is often the first impression a buyer has of your brand. A sloppy or incomplete listing signals that you're not retail-ready, while a polished one builds trust and interest.

Product Photography

Must-Have: High-resolution images of packaging (front, back, side)

Bonus: Lifestyle shots showing the product in use (ex., snack bar on a hiking trail, beverage being poured)

Pro Tip: Use a white background for your main image, most platforms require this.

Product Details

RangeMe: Case pack, MSRP, certifications (organic, non-GMO, kosher, etc.), shelf life.

Mable: Order minimums, shipping times, and regional sourcing notes.

Faire: Suggested retail price, reorder rates, and whether the product is "giftable."

Pricing and Terms

RangeMe: Align pricing with distributor-readiness (FOB, wholesale).

Mable: Set fair MOQs (minimum order quantities) for independents; too high discourages trial.

Faire: Highlight flexible terms (net 60, free shipping promos), this is a key draw for their buyers.

Certifications and Proof Points

- Upload every certification you have, USDA Organic, Non-GMO, Gluten-Free, etc.

- Highlight press mentions, awards, or velocity data if available.

- On RangeMe especially, certifications improve visibility in buyer searches.

Updates and Engagement

- Refresh your profile quarterly with new photos, SKUs, or awards.

- Check analytics (available on Mable and Faire) to see where traction is building.

- Respond quickly to buyer inquiries, delays = lost trust.

Typical Retail Vendor Set Up Process

Getting a "yes" from a retailer is only the beginning. Before your product hits shelves, you must go through the vendor set up process, the behind-the-scenes paperwork, and compliance steps that make you an official supplier. This process can feel tedious and overwhelming for first-time founders, but it's critical to get it right. Mistakes or delays at this stage can push back your launch or even jeopardize your relationship with the retailer.

What the Vendor Set Up Process Includes

Vendor Application / Onboarding Forms

Retailers require detailed forms with company information, product details, and compliance documentation.

Be ready to provide:

- Business license, tax ID, W-9
- Insurance certificates (general liability, product liability)
- Banking details for ACH payments
- Contact information for key staff

. . .

Product Information Management (PIM) / New Item Form

Each SKU requires its own form with:

- UPC/EAN codes
- Case pack, weights, and dimensions
- Shelf life and storage requirements
- Certifications (organic, non-GMO, gluten-free, etc.)
- Marketing claims (and substantiation if required)

EDI (Electronic Data Interchange) Set Up

Many retailers require EDI for order processing and invoicing. This often means working with a third-party EDI provider.

Pro Tip: Budget for set up and monthly EDI fees, they can be $100–$500/month.

Insurance Requirements

- Retailers typically require proof of product liability insurance, with them named as an additional insured.
- Some may require higher coverage limits than you expected (often $2M+ aggregate).

Compliance Documentation

- Retailers may ask for safety certifications, FDA compliance letters, or allergen statements.
- Perishable or imported products may also require HACCP plans or import documentation.

Logistics and Routing Guides

- You'll receive a routing guide with shipping and packaging specifications.
- Includes pallet standards, labeling, appointment scheduling, and chargeback policies.
- Non-compliance = fines or refused shipments.

Payment Terms

- Standard terms are Net 30, but many retailers push to Net 45, 60, or even 90 days.
- Be prepared to manage cash flow while waiting for payments.

Vendor Portal Access

- Once approved, you'll gain access to the retailer's online portal for managing orders, invoices, and compliance documents.
- Staying on top of this portal is critical to keeping your account in good standing.

Key Decision Makers in Grocery Retail

Getting your product onto store shelves, and keeping it there, depends on understanding who actually makes decisions inside grocery retail. It's a layered ecosystem, and success comes from knowing not just who to talk to, but how to frame your pitch around what each role cares about. When founders miss this, they often waste time pitching the wrong person or emphasizing the wrong priorities.

Buyers

Buyers are usually the first and most visible gatekeepers. They are responsible for deciding which products are listed within a specific category or department, and they juggle hundreds of SKUs at any given time. Buyers focus heavily on pricing, margins, promotional support, and whether your product fits their shopper profile. They also look for proof of demand, whether that's velocity data, strong local performance, or clear consumer pull. Because their time is limited, buyers respond best to pitches that are concise, data-informed, and clearly answer the question: why does this product deserve space on my shelf?

. . .

Category Managers

Category managers operate at a broader level, especially within larger retail organizations. While smaller retailers may combine the buyer and category manager roles, larger chains separate them. Category managers oversee the health of an entire category and are measured on growth, profitability, and long-term strategy. They care less about individual brand stories and more about how a product fills white space, aligns with trends, or attracts new shoppers. Founders who can speak the language of category growth, rather than just product features, are far more likely to earn serious consideration.

Category Captains

Category captains add another layer of influence. These are typically large, established manufacturers that partner with retailers to provide data, insights, and planograms for a category. While they don't make final decisions, their recommendations often shape assortments and shelf layouts. Category captains are focused on maintaining leadership and protecting share, which means they can be both a source of insight and a competitive force. Knowing who the category captain is in your space helps you understand the dynamics at play and anticipate potential resistance or support.

Merchandising

Merchandising teams are responsible for execution on the ground. They ensure products are set according to planograms, displays are built correctly, and promotions are executed as intended. Even the best buyer decision CEO can fail if merchandising breaks down. Late deliveries, incorrect case packs, or unclear instructions can result in poor placement or missed displays, directly impacting sales. Founders who respect this function and make execution easy often see stronger in-store results.

. . .

Store Managers

Store managers, while not typically involved in category-wide decisions, have meaningful influence at the store level. They care about smooth operations, fast-selling products, and happy customers. In many cases, store managers can advocate internally for products that perform well locally or ensure better shelf placement and replenishment. Building relationships here, especially in early or regional launches, can materially improve outcomes.

Distributors and Brokers

Distributors and brokers, while not retailers themselves, are critical gatekeepers in the process. Distributors focus on consistent ordering, clean logistics, and reliable velocity, while brokers concentrate on selling your product into accounts and managing buyer relationships. Both care deeply about brands that are easy to work with, well-prepared, and supportive of promotions. When these partners are confident in your execution, they become allies rather than obstacles.

Understanding how all of these roles fit together allows founders to pitch more strategically, align expectations, and navigate retail with far less friction. When you tailor your message to each decision-maker's priorities, you move from simply asking for shelf space to earning it.

A strong distributor or broker relationship often opens the door to buyers. Don't treat them as middlemen, treat them as partners.

Retail decisions are rarely made by just one person. Success requires knowing who holds the keys at each stage, and tailoring your message to their priorities. Buyers care about margin, category managers care about growth, captains care about leadership, and store managers care about execution.

Pro Tip: Map out the decision-makers for each retailer you target. Knowing who's who, and what they value, turns a cold pitch into a strategic conversation.

PRESENTING YOUR PRODUCTS

Once you've secured a meeting with a buyer or category manager, the next step is delivering a professional, concise, and persuasive presentation. This is your opportunity to prove not just that your product is great, but that it deserves a spot on their shelves and can perform in their category.

Retailers expect a structured pitch that covers key areas: your brand story, your product assortment, your pricing, sales proof points, and your promotional strategy. If you walk in unprepared, you risk burning an opportunity that may not come around again for another year.

Your Selling Deck

What It Is:
Your selling deck (sometimes called a "sell sheet" or "presentation deck") is your primary leave-behind with the buyer. It should be professional, branded, and easy to digest.

What to Include:

- Brand story (short and compelling)
- Mission and point of differentiation
- Product photos and assortment overview
- Certifications (organic, non-GMO, etc.)
- Proof of demand (velocity data, consumer testimonials)
- Pricing strategy

- Promotional plans

Pro Tip: Keep it to 10–12 slides max. Buyers don't have time for long decks — clarity and impact matter most.

Assortment

What It Is:
A clear presentation of the products you're offering, including flavors, pack sizes, and formats.

Best Practices:

- Don't overwhelm the buyer with your entire portfolio, start with 2–3 SKUs that represent your best-sellers or strongest innovations.
- Highlight what makes each SKU unique and relevant to the retailer's shopper base.
- Show how your assortment fits within the category (white space, trend alignment).

Pricing Strategy

What It Is:
Your wholesale pricing, case pack, MSRP, and margin structure.

Best Practices:

- Demonstrate that you understand the retailer's pricing expectations for the category.
- Be transparent about how you arrived at your pricing.
- Show that you've factored in trade spend and allowances.
- Clearly state both unit pricing and case pricing.

Historical Sales Data / Velocities

What It Is:
Proof that your product sells where it's already available.

Best Practices:

- Present units sold per store per week (UPSPW) or velocities, the metric most buyers trust.
- If you're too early for syndicated data, share results from DTC, farmers markets, or local independents.
- Highlight repeat purchase rates if you have them.

Pro Tip: Buyers want reassurance that their shelf space won't go to waste. Velocity data is the best way to prove it.

Your Projections

What It Is:
Your estimate of how your product will perform if given placement.

Best Practices:

- Base projections on realistic assumptions (don't claim you'll outsell Pepsi in year one).
- Align your forecast with category norms (look at competitive benchmarks).
- Show both conservative and stretch scenarios.
- Demonstrate that you understand seasonality if relevant (ex., BBQ sauces peaking in summer).

Your Promotions (TPRs, IRCs, BOGOs, Scan Downs, Coupons)

What It Is:
Your promotional strategy, the planned discounts and incentives you'll fund to drive trial and repeat.

Types to Highlight:

- **TPRs (Temporary Price Reductions):** Short-term shelf price discounts.
- **IRCs (Instant Redeemable Coupons):** Stickers or on-pack coupons for immediate savings.
- **BOGOs (Buy One Get One):** Classic trial driver.
- **Scan Downs:** Discounts applied at the register when scanned.
- **Coupons:** Digital, print, or app-based offers.

Best Practices:

- Show that you've thought through an annual or quarterly promotional calendar.
- Budget realistically, promotions cost money, but they're essential to build velocity.
- Demonstrate flexibility to participate in retailer-specific programs.

A polished presentation demonstrates that you're not just a passionate founder, but a professional partner who understands how retail works. Buyers don't just evaluate your product; they evaluate *you*. A clear, confident pitch signals that you'll be easy to work with and prepared to support your product once it's on shelf.

Pro Tip: Practice your pitch in front of advisors or mentors before presenting to a retailer. Buyers appreciate founders who are enthusiastic but also prepared with the data and plans that prove retail readiness.

Your Salesforce

No matter how great your product is, it won't sell itself. In the food industry, sales are a contact sport, built on relationships, persistence, and credibility. Having a sales team that is knowledgeable, confident, and dedicated is not optional; it's essential.

A strong salesforce does more than just pitch your product. They:

- **Build Relationships:** With buyers, distributors, and brokers, relationships that can open doors or keep them closed.

- **Tell Your Story:** Translating your brand vision into a compelling pitch that resonates with gatekeepers.

- **Handle Objections:** Buyers will have concerns about pricing, logistics, or velocity; your team must know how to address them.

- **Drive Execution:** Securing meetings, following up on leads, ensuring compliance with retailer requirements, and monitoring sell-through.

- **Provide Feedback:** Sales teams are often the first to hear what's working (and what's not) in the market.

For startups, the sales team doesn't need to be huge, but it does need to be strategic, committed, and aligned with the company's goals. Many founders underestimate how much time and energy selling requires. Even the most mission-driven food company needs someone out there pounding the pavement, talking to buyers, and closing deals.

Why a Dedicated Salesforce Matters

A dedicated salesforce is one of the clearest signals that a brand is ready to operate at a professional level. Retail buyers and distributors expect to work with partners who treat selling as a core business function, not a side task squeezed between production runs and social media posts. When a brand shows up with a consistent, knowledgeable sales presence, it communicates seriousness, reliability, and respect for the buyer's time.

Sales also requires sustained focus, something many founders struggle to maintain while juggling product development, operations, and marketing. Dedicated salespeople ensure leads are followed up on, meetings are scheduled, and opportunities don't quietly fade away. Buyers frequently point to follow-through as the deciding factor between brands that land accounts and those that don't. While marketing may spark interest, sales is what converts that interest into real distribution. Without an intentional sales engine in place, even the most talked-about brand can find its growth stalled on the sidelines.

Types of Startup Sales Teams

Startups have options when it comes to building a salesforce. Each structure comes with trade-offs in cost, control, and reach. The most common models include:

- **In-House Sales (Internal)**
- **Broker Networks (External)**

We'll break each of these down in the subsections that follow, when they make sense, how much they cost, and what founders should watch out for.

Pro Tip: Sales is the most expensive line item many startups overlook. Whether it's your time as a founder or the cost of hiring, someone *must* be accountable for driving revenue. If you don't invest in sales, your competition will.

Founder-Led Sales

Founder-led sales is the reality for most food brands at the very beginning. In this stage, the founder personally handles selling, pitching buyers, dropping off samples, following up on emails, and sometimes even delivering cases to stores. It's rarely glamorous work, but it's foundational. This hands-on approach is often the first real test of whether a product and brand can gain traction beyond friends, family, and early supporters.

Founders typically start here out of necessity. Early-stage brands rarely have the cash to hire sales reps or brokers, making founder-led sales the most practical option. Just as importantly, no one can tell the brand story with more conviction than the founder. Buyers respond to that authenticity and passion, especially when evaluating new or unproven products. Direct conversations with buyers also create a powerful learning loop, exposing objections, pricing concerns, and merchandising challenges in real time. That feedback is invaluable and can shape everything from packaging to positioning.

Finally, founder involvement signals commitment. Retailers and distributors are far more likely to take a chance on a brand when they see the founder fully invested in making the business work.

Pros:

- Deep connection with buyers, they meet the person behind the brand.
- No additional payroll or commission costs.
- Accelerates your learning about pricing, objections, and what resonates.
- Builds credibility with early retail partners ("the founder is hustling").

Cons:

- Time-consuming, every hour spent selling is an hour not spent on operations, marketing, or product development.
- Limited bandwidth, you can't cover wide geographies or multiple channels alone.
- Professionalism gap, some retailers may expect a polished sales team and question if you're ready.
- Emotional fatigue, rejection feels more personal when you *are* the sales team.

Cost Considerations:

- Direct costs are low (samples, travel, booth fees), but the opportunity cost of your time is high.
- You'll still need to budget for trade spend, demos, and collateral, being the salesperson doesn't eliminate those expenses.

Pro Tip: Founder-led sales is a rite of passage. Even if you later hire brokers or build an in-house team, starting here helps you understand the process, refine your pitch, and build the credibility you'll need with future partners.

When It Works Best:

- **Early Validation Stage:** Farmers markets, local independents, regional co-ops.
- **Proof of Concept:** To build data that justifies engaging brokers or hiring reps.
- **Cash-Strapped Startups:** When funds simply don't allow for dedicated sales staff.

Pro Tip: Document everything you learn in founder-led sales, common objections, buyer questions, margins that get pushback, SKUs that perform best. This "sales playbook" will become invaluable once you hand off to an in-house team or broker.

In-House Sales (Internal)

In-house sales refers to building an internal sales team made up of employees who work exclusively for your company. These team members are fully embedded in your brand, your culture, and your day-to-day operations. Because they represent only your products, they develop deep knowledge of your positioning, pricing, and priorities, and they carry that clarity into every buyer conversation.

Founders often choose this model when they want greater control and consistency in how the brand shows up in the market. An internal team can be trained to deliver a very specific sales narrative, ensuring that retailers and distributors hear the same story every time. Over repeated interactions, this consistency builds trust. In-house sales teams also create a tight feedback loop, since they are closely connected to operations, marketing, and leadership.

Insights from buyers can be shared quickly and acted on in real time. Unlike brokers who juggle multiple brands, internal salespeople are fully dedicated to driving your business forward.

In early-stage startups, this structure usually evolves gradually. The founder often remains deeply involved in sales while hiring the first dedicated representative. As the business grows, this may expand into a small team that includes a sales lead or director, regional account managers focused on key territories, and eventually inside sales support to manage smaller accounts and ongoing follow-up. Even a lean in-house team can significantly increase capacity while allowing the founder to step back from day-to-day selling without losing control of the sales process.

Pros:

- Full-time dedication to your brand.
- Strong alignment between sales, marketing, and operations.
- Better relationship management, buyers often prefer consistent reps.
- Easier to train on compliance, systems, and your unique brand voice.

Cons:

- **Expensive:** Salaries, benefits, travel, and commissions quickly add up.
- **Limited Reach:** One or two internal reps can't cover the entire U.S. efficiently.
- **Slow Ramp:** Building an internal team takes time and requires training.
- **Founder Dependency:** In small teams, the founder often still carries heavy sales responsibilities.

Cost Considerations:

- **Base Salary:** Entry-level sales rep $50K–$65K; experienced account manager $75K–$100K+.
- **Benefits and Taxes:** Add ~25–30% on top of salary for health, payroll, and retirement contributions.
- **Travel:** $10K–$20K annually per rep for flights, hotels, meals, and trade shows.
- **Commissions/Bonuses:** 5–10% of sales or performance-based bonuses.

Pro Tip: In-house sales is often best once your brand has proven velocity and stable distribution. At the very early stage, this model may be too costly, but as you scale, it provides unmatched consistency and brand control.

Brokers (External)

Brokers are independent sales representatives or agencies that sell your product on your behalf as external partners. They typically represent multiple brands at the same time and are paid on commission rather than salary, making them contractors rather than employees. Because they are not embedded within your company, brokers operate as an extension of your sales effort rather than a fully integrated team.

Founders often turn to brokers as a way to access the market more quickly and cost-effectively, especially in the early stages. Since brokers already have established relationships with buyers, they can open doors that might take a founder months or years to unlock alone. This can be particularly valuable when entering new regions or channels where you lack visibility. Brokers also bring practical expertise, including familiarity with category reviews, retailer portals, and compliance requirements, which can reduce costly missteps.

In practice, working with a broker involves signing an agreement that defines the territory or accounts they cover and the commission they will earn, typically in the 5–7% range, though it can be higher for emerging brands. Brokers present your product to buyers, manage submissions, and support follow-up, but they are not a turnkey solution. The brand is still responsible for marketing support, samples, trade spend, pricing strategy, and distributor coordination. Brokers can accelerate access, but success depends on how well the founder supports and manages the relationship.

Pros:

- No fixed payroll costs; you only pay when they sell.
- Faster introductions through their existing buyer network.
- Scalable, you can engage brokers in multiple regions without hiring a national team.
- Helpful for categories where relationships drive placement (snacks, beverages, natural/organic).

Cons:

- **Divided Attention:** Brokers represent multiple brands; your product may not always be their top priority.
- **Less Control:** You can't dictate how they present your brand as tightly as you could with employees.
- **Ongoing Management Required:** You still need to hold them accountable, track activity, and support them with marketing tools.
- **Hidden Costs:** Even with commission-only models, you must still cover samples, trade show presence, and promotional allowances.

Cost Considerations:

- **Commission:** Typically 5–7% of sales, sometimes 10% for early-stage brands.
- **Retainers (Occasional):** Some brokers charge a small monthly retainer plus commission, especially if your brand is unproven.
- **Trade Spend Still Yours:** Retailer promotions, distributor fees, and samples are not included in the broker fee.

Pro Tip: Don't confuse brokers with distributors. Brokers don't take ownership of your product, they just sell it. You are still responsible for fulfillment, logistics, and ensuring the product moves.

Hybrid Model

A hybrid sales model blends multiple approaches, most often combining founder-led or in-house sales with external brokers or agencies. Instead of choosing a single structure, this model allows brands to design a sales engine that matches their stage, budget, and growth priorities. Many successful food startups evolve into a hybrid model because it offers a practical balance between reach and control.

Founders are drawn to this approach because it scales without forcing an all-or-nothing decision. Internal staff or the founder can stay closely involved with the most strategic relationships, while brokers extend coverage into additional regions or channels that would otherwise be difficult or expensive to reach. This structure also allows for flexibility over time, as regions that prove profitable can gradually be brought in-house, while brokers continue to support emerging or lower-priority markets. From a cost perspective, it limits fixed payroll expenses while still ensuring consistent sales momentum.

In practice, the hybrid model often looks like the founder or a small internal sales team managing key accounts such as regional grocery chains or priority natural retailers. Brokers are then engaged to cover outlying territories, independent stores, or regions where they already have strong buyer relationships. A centralized sales coordinator or inside sales function typically supports both groups, maintaining CRM systems, tracking leads, and ensuring follow-up doesn't fall through the cracks. When managed well, the hybrid model delivers broad coverage without sacrificing focus or accountability.

Pros:

- Best of both worlds: control over strategy plus reach in new regions.
- Allows faster expansion than a founder-only or in-house-only model.
- Can be adjusted over time, expand in-house presence as revenue grows.
- Brokers provide introductions; internal reps build deeper relationships.

Cons:

- Requires strong management and accountability systems to avoid overlap or miscommunication between in-house and brokers.
- Complexity increases, multiple contracts, commission structures, and priorities to juggle.
- Risk of channel conflict if responsibilities aren't clearly defined.
- Costs can creep up if not carefully monitored (commissions + salaries).

Cost Considerations:

- **Internal Sales Staff:** Salary + benefits + travel (as outlined in in-house section).
- **Broker Commission:** Typically 5–7% in assigned territories.
- **Sales Coordinator/Admin Support:** $40K–$60K annually if added.
- **Tools:** CRM software is almost a must in hybrid models to track who's calling on which accounts.

Hybrid works best once your brand has traction in 1–2 regions and is expanding into new geographies or channels. It lets you invest where you're strong while "renting" coverage where you're not.

Pro Tip: Success in a hybrid model comes down to clarity of roles. Put in writing which accounts are owned by the in-house team vs. brokers, how leads are assigned, and how performance is measured. Ambiguity creates friction.

BONUS - CUSTOMER RELATIONSHIP MANAGEMENT (CRM)

Customer Relationship Management, or CRM, is both a system and a mindset for managing relationships with buyers, distributors, brokers, and, in some cases, consumers. At its most basic level, CRM is a digital tool that tracks your sales pipeline, who you've contacted, what was discussed, what's been promised, and what still needs follow-up. In practice, it becomes the shared memory of your sales operation, replacing scattered spreadsheets, inbox searches, and half-remembered conversations with a single, organized source of truth.

For founders, CRM quickly becomes essential as conversations multiply. Every retailer, distributor, or broker contact can live in one place, complete with notes, emails, meeting history, and next steps, so nothing gets lost over time. It also introduces accountability into the sales process. Follow-up is often the difference between winning placement and being forgotten, and CRM creates reminders and structure that ensure commitments are met and opportunities don't slip through the cracks. As the business grows, this structure allows accounts to be handed off smoothly to brokers or new hires without losing valuable relationship history, while also making it easier to track performance metrics such as open opportunities, win rates, and sales cycle length.

There are CRM tools well suited to early-stage brands, including affordable or free options like HubSpot CRM, Zoho, and Pipedrive, as well as food-industry-friendly platforms such as Crisp, Repsly, or more robust systems like Salesforce. Very early on, a thoughtfully designed spreadsheet can serve as a lightweight stand-in, but only temporarily. The real value of any CRM comes from consistent use. Logging calls, updating notes, and reviewing dashboards regularly is what turns the system into a growth tool rather than just another piece of software.

Once you're juggling multiple buyers, a CRM system is no longer optional.

Category Management

Category management is one of the most important, and most misunderstood, concepts in retail. At its core, it's the framework retailers use to organize, evaluate, and grow an entire section of the store, whether that's salty snacks, plant-based beverages, or frozen meals. Buyers don't look at your product in isolation. They evaluate it through the lens of how it will impact the overall performance of the category they manage. For founders, understanding this mindset is essential. When you learn to think like a category manager, you stop selling a product and start offering a solution that helps the retailer grow sales, margin, and relevance.

In practice, category management is how retailers decide what stays on the shelf and what comes off. Category managers group products into logical sets, analyze sales data and consumer trends, monitor competitor performance, and make decisions about assortment, pricing, promotions, and shelf space. They are often described as the "mini-CEOs" of their categories because they are accountable for hitting growth and profitability targets. Every new SKU they add must earn its place by contributing to those goals.

This is why category management matters so much for founders. Retailers aren't just asking whether your product tastes good, they're asking whether it strengthens the category. Shelf space is limited, and adding one item often means removing another. Buyers rely heavily on data such as velocity, margins, and trend alignment to guide those decisions. Even early-stage brands can participate in this conversation by bringing thoughtful insights from local accounts, direct-to-consumer sales, or consumer feedback. Strong positioning and storytelling also play a role, especially when you can clearly articulate how your product fills a gap, attracts a new shopper, or brings innovation to a tired set.

When evaluating new products, category managers tend to focus on a few consistent questions. They want to know whether an item is incremental, bringing in new shoppers rather than simply shifting sales from an existing brand. They assess whether it aligns with current or emerging trends, whether the financials support required margins and promotions, and whether there is credible proof of performance, even at a small scale. Fit matters too, including packaging, price point, and size relative to the retailer's shopper base.

Founders who understand category management can use it to their advantage. Studying the shelf reveals who is winning, what's overrepresented, and where white space exists. A strong pitch frames the product as category-expanding rather than just "better." Bringing even modest data points shows seriousness and preparation. Most importantly, approaching the relationship as a partnership changes the dynamic. The consumer may be the end customer, but the buyer is your collaborator in growing the category. When you help them succeed, you dramatically increase your chances of earning, and keeping, your place on the shelf.

Pro Tip: Never walk into a category manager meeting saying, "My product is better." Instead, walk in with a clear answer to: *"How will my product grow your category?"* That's the language buyers speak.

Category Review

Category review is one of the most important, and unknown, activity that founders encounter and fail to plan for. It's the formal process retailers use to evaluate how a category is performing and decide which products stay, which are removed, and which new items are added. For founders, understanding how category reviews work is critical because many retailers only consider new products once, or at most twice, a year. If your timing is off, even a strong product can sit on the sidelines for 12 months, with real consequences for forecasting, production, and cash flow.

Timing is what gives category reviews their power. Retailers plan far in advance, aligning reviews with broader merchandising strategies and shelf resets. If you're building a sales forecast that assumes a retailer launch this year, but their next review isn't until the following spring, your numbers will be unrealistic from the start. Missing a review cycle doesn't just slow growth, it can push a launch back an entire year. This is why buyers are rarely receptive to mid-cycle pitches. They want innovation presented in sync with their planning windows, not on an ad hoc basis.

Behind the scenes, category reviews are structured and data-driven. Most categories are reviewed annually, though faster-moving categories like beverages or snacks may be reviewed twice a year. Retailers often require formal submissions months in advance, typically through vendor portals or platforms like RangeMe. During the review, buyers assess sales performance, velocity, margins, trend alignment, and how each product fits into the retailer's overall strategy. Once decisions are finalized, planograms are reset and new assortments roll out during specific, tightly scheduled reset periods.

For founders, the implications are significant. You should never assume new retail business will materialize in the same year unless you are already confirmed for a category review. Production planning needs to stay conservative until approvals are secured, and cash flow projections should account for the possibility of delayed launches. Perhaps most importantly, patience is required. A "no" often isn't about your product, it's about timing, and that's a normal part of the retail process.

One simple habit can change everything: ask every buyer you meet when their next category review is for your category. That single question tells you when to submit, when decisions will be made, and how to align your forecasts and launch plans. Over time, building and maintaining a master list of category review calendars across your target retailers becomes one of the most valuable planning tools in your business.

Pro Tip: Treat category review calendars like gold. Build a master list of review periods for your target retailers. It will become one of the most valuable sales planning tools in your company.

BONUS - OBTAINING RETAILER CATEGORY REVIEW CALENDARS

Knowing when retailers review categories is one of the most powerful tools in a founder's toolkit. But those dates aren't always publicly available, and every retailer has their own process. Getting access to review calendars takes persistence, networking, and strategy.

How to Obtain Review Calendars

Ask Buyers Directly

- The simplest and most reliable method. When meeting or emailing a buyer, ask:
  - *"When is your next review for [category]?"*

- Buyers are accustomed to this question; it shows you're serious and understand the process.

Distributor and Broker Partners

- Distributors like UNFI and KeHE, or experienced brokers, often have internal knowledge of review cycles.

- Leverage these relationships, they may share timing or remind you when submissions are due.

Vendor Portals

- Many large retailers (ex., Kroger, Walmart, Target) provide online vendor portals with timelines, submission guidelines, and review periods.

- Once you're an approved vendor or have applied through platforms like RangeMe, you may gain access.

Trade Associations and Industry Groups

- Organizations like FMI (Food Industry Association), Specialty Food Association, or regional grocer associations sometimes share review calendars with members.

- Membership fees can be worth it for access and networking.

Industry Networks

- Fellow founders, sales reps, and mentors often share insights informally.

- Attending trade shows, conferences, or networking events is a good way to gather intelligence.

Category Captains (Big Brands)

- In some categories, large manufacturers act as "category captains" and help manage retailer planograms. While they may not share full calendars, their activity (ex., big reset promotions) often signals when reviews happen.

Helpful Tips

- **Build a Calendar:** Even if you don't have every date, start building a spreadsheet with what you know. Over time, you'll fill in the blanks.

- **Plan Backwards:** If a review is in June, submissions may be due by March. Always confirm lead times.

- **Stay Proactive:** Don't wait to be told. Ask early, and confirm dates at least twice a year.

Pro Tip: Treat review calendars like an evolving playbook. They may shift slightly year to year, but once you track them, you'll always know when to pitch, when to budget promotions, and how to forecast with confidence.

Vendor Allowances

Vendor allowances are payments, discounts, or credits that suppliers provide to retailers for specific purposes tied to placement, promotion, or distribution. While the structures vary by retailer and agreement, allowances are a standard part of doing business in grocery and mass retail. They are not optional line items or "nice-to-haves", they are built into how retailers manage risk, fund promotions, and move product through their systems.

Allowances can take several forms. Slotting fees are typically one-time charges required to place a new product on shelf and can range from a few thousand dollars at independents to six figures at major national chains. Promotional allowances fund temporary price reductions such as BOGOs, scan-downs, or endcap features and are usually planned in advance as part of a retailer's annual or quarterly promotion calendar. Advertising, often called co-op marketing allowances, support retailer-led marketing like circulars, digital ads, or loyalty programs. Many retailers also require a damages or unsaleables allowance, usually one to three percent of gross sales, to offset returns, spoilage, or expired product. Distribution center allowances cover the cost of warehousing, handling, or processing product through a retailer's DC network, while new item introductory allowances may include discounted pricing or free cases to encourage initial placement of a new SKU.

For founders, vendor allowances matter because they directly impact profitability and cash flow. These costs are often overlooked early on, but they can quietly erode margins if they're not forecasted and built into pricing from the start. With most large retailers, allowances are simply part of the cost of access, and opting out is rarely an option. Buyers expect them and view participation as a sign that a brand understands retail economics and is prepared to support the category. When planned intentionally, allowances become a strategic tool rather than a surprise expense, helping you enter retail relationships with clear expectations and a more sustainable financial model.

Pro Tip: Always model vendor allowances into your cost of doing business before you sign with a retailer. Don't get caught celebrating a big win in distribution only to realize the economics don't work once allowances are factored in.

Fees and Deductions

Getting into distribution and onto retail shelves is never just about the cost of making your product. Beyond COGS, trade spend, and ongoing vendor allowances, there are standard entry fees that most distributors and retailers require simply to do business. These fees are easy to overlook when you're early in the process, but they can materially affect your launch budget and cash flow. Understanding them before you sign contracts helps you avoid surprises and make realistic commitments about where and how fast you can expand.

Slotting Fees: The Cost of Getting on Shelf

Slotting fees are the most well-known, and often the most intimidating, costs in the CPG industry. For many first-time founders, this is the moment where the realities of retail become clear. Up until this point, the focus has been on product, brand, and demand. Slotting introduces a different dimension, access.

At its core, slotting is a one-time payment made to a retailer to secure shelf space for a new product. It compensates the retailer for the risk of removing an existing item to make room for yours. Every shelf is a revenue-generating asset, and when a retailer replaces a proven product with a new one, they are taking a calculated risk. Slotting is how that risk is shared.

These fees can be assessed in several ways. They may be charged per SKU, per store, per region, or as part of a broader rollout program. The structure depends on the retailer and the scope of distribution. Independent stores may charge only a few hundred dollars, making them an accessible entry point for emerging brands. Regional chains can range from $5,000 to $25,000 per SKU, while national chains may require six-figure investments for broad placement across hundreds or thousands of stores.

What often surprises founders is not just the size of the fee, but the scale. Slotting is rarely a single check tied to a single store. It multiplies quickly as distribution expands. A product placed in 1,000 stores at even a modest fee per store can result in a significant upfront investment before a single unit is sold. This is why slotting is one of the most common points where early-stage brands overextend themselves financially.

It is also important to understand what slotting does and does not do. Slotting secures access to the shelf, but it does not guarantee performance. Once the product is placed, it must still meet velocity expectations. If it underperforms, it may be discontinued during the next reset cycle, regardless of the initial investment. In that sense, slotting is an entry fee, not an insurance policy.

In some cases, slotting can be negotiated, reduced, or replaced with alternative forms of investment. Retailers may waive or lower fees if there is strong consumer demand, proven sales data from other accounts, or a compelling promotional plan. Brands may also offer free fill, increased trade support, or marketing commitments in lieu of a traditional slotting fee. These negotiations are more likely when a brand can demonstrate that it will drive traffic and sales, not just occupy space.

For founders, the key is to plan for slotting early and approach it strategically. It should be built into your launch budget, reflected in your pricing model, and aligned with your expected return. Just as important, founders should resist the temptation to scale too quickly.

Expanding into more stores than your budget and support systems can sustain is one of the fastest ways to create financial strain.

For better or worse, slotting is part of the cost of doing business in retail. It sits alongside other access-related costs such as listing fees, system onboarding, and compliance requirements. Many first-time founders underestimate these expenses, but retailers and distributors rely on them as part of their operating model.

Core Trade and Operational Deductions

These deductions are most directly tied to selling activity and day-to-day operations. They are often expected and should be built into your pricing and forecasting from the beginning.

Trade Promotions (Scans, BOGOs, Promos, Ads)

Retail promotions are a primary driver of sales, but they come at a cost. Temporary price reductions, buy-one-get-one offers, and advertised promotions are typically funded by the brand. These costs are often deducted after the promotion runs based on actual units sold or agreed-upon allowances.

Billbacks

Billbacks occur when a retailer or distributor deducts funds from your invoice to cover agreed-upon programs, most commonly trade promotions. While they are legitimate when aligned with prior agreements, they must be carefully tracked to ensure accuracy.

Off-Invoice Discounts

These are upfront discounts applied directly to your invoice, reducing the amount the customer pays at the time of purchase. While simpler to track than billbacks, they still reduce your net revenue and must be accounted for in your pricing structure.

·   ·   ·

EDI Non-Compliance Charges

Retailers require strict adherence to Electronic Data Interchange (EDI) standards for orders, invoices, and shipping notices. Errors or delays can trigger fees, even if the issue is administrative. These charges can add up quickly if systems are not properly managed.

Shortage Deductions

If a retailer or distributor claims that fewer units were received than invoiced, they may deduct the difference. These claims are not always accurate, making it important to maintain strong documentation and dispute processes.

Damaged Goods

Products that arrive damaged or become unsellable in the supply chain may be deducted from your payment. Depending on the agreement, this may fall partially or fully on the brand.

Other Fees and Deductions to Plan For

Beyond core trade activity, there are additional financial adjustments that can impact cash flow and profitability. Some are predictable, while others depend on the specific retailer, distributor, or contract terms.

Marketing Fund Deductions

Some retailers require brands to contribute to a shared marketing fund, which supports in-store signage, circulars, or broader promotional efforts. These are often deducted as a percentage of sales.

Returns

Unsold or discontinued products may be returned to the brand, particularly in certain channels. This can result in both lost revenue and additional costs related to handling or disposal.

2/10 Net 30 (Early Pay Discounts)

Some customers take early payment discounts, such as 2% off if paid within 10 days, even when operating on longer payment terms. This reduces your collected revenue and should be factored into your financial model.

New Vendor Holds (60–90 Days)

New suppliers are often subject to extended payment holds during onboarding. This delays cash collection beyond standard terms and can place additional strain on working capital.

Guaranteed Sales Agreements

In some cases, brands agree to guarantee sales performance. If products do not meet agreed-upon thresholds, the brand may be responsible for covering the shortfall or buying back inventory.

Spoilage (Capped or Uncapped)

Perishable products may be subject to spoilage allowances. Depending on the agreement, the brand may absorb a percentage of unsold or expired product, either with a cap or without one.

Freight Allowances

Retailers may require the brand to contribute to or fully cover freight costs. This may be structured as a fixed allowance or built into pricing expectations.

· · ·

Freight Detention Fees

Delays during delivery, such as missed appointments or extended unloading times, can result in detention charges from carriers. These are often passed back to the brand.

Deduction Authorization

Not all deductions should be accepted at face value. While many fees are part of standard retail operations, each deduction must be tied to a prior agreement, program, or valid operational issue. This is where deduction authorization becomes critical.

Deduction authorization refers to the process of validating whether a retailer or distributor has the right to take a deduction from your invoice. In practice, this means confirming that the deduction aligns with agreed-upon trade promotions, contract terms, pricing structures, or documented supply chain events. Without this validation step, brands risk absorbing unnecessary or incorrect charges that erode margins over time.

A disciplined approach includes maintaining clear records of all trade agreements, promotional calendars, pricing terms, and shipping documentation. When a deduction appears, it should be matched against these records to confirm accuracy. If the deduction cannot be substantiated, it should be disputed promptly with supporting documentation.

Over time, this process becomes a critical financial control. Even small discrepancies, when repeated across multiple accounts or shipments, can add up to meaningful losses. Founders who actively manage deduction authorization not only protect their revenue, but also signal professionalism and operational maturity to their retail partners.

In one client engagement, I saw firsthand just how costly and overwhelming deduction management can become. The company had accumulated such a large volume of unresolved retailer deductions that we ultimately hired an accounting contractor to spend nearly three months auditing and organizing the claims. After carefully reviewing the records against promotional agreements, invoices, freight documentation, and contractual terms, we discovered that nearly 40% of the deductions were unauthorized or inaccurate. By formally disputing and documenting those claims, well over six figures were successfully recouped.

Authorization	Deduction
Typically Authorized	Trade (Scans, BOGOs, Promos, Ads)
Typically Authorized	Bill backs
Typically Authorized	Off Invoice
Contractual	EDI Non-Compliant Charge
Contractual	Shortage Deduction
Typically Unauthorized	Damaged Goods
Contractual	2/10 Net 30
Contractual	New Vendor Holds (60-90 days)
Contractual	Guaranteed Sales Agreement
Typically Unauthorized	Spoilage (% capped or not)
Contractual	Freight Allowance
Typically Unauthorized	Freight Detention Fees

Table: Common Deductions

Key Takeaway

Fees and deductions are not exceptions, they are part of the financial structure of the CPG industry. There's no way to avoid them, so be prepared to anticipate, track, and manage them effectively.

Founders who understand these dynamics can:
- Build more accurate pricing models
- Forecast net revenue instead of gross assumptions
- Identify and dispute invalid deductions
- Protect margins as they scale

Ignoring these costs can create a disconnect between expected and actual performance. Understanding them ensures that your business reflects reality, not just projections.

BONUS - DEDUCTION MANAGEMENT

One of the least glamorous, but most critical, aspects of working with retailers is managing deductions. While some deductions are standard and predictable, others can spiral into a mountain of paperwork, surprise charges, and disputes. Left unchecked, deductions can erode margins to the point where profitable sales become loss-making.

Why Deduction Management Matters

- **Volume of Deductions:** As your business grows, the number of invoices, chargebacks, promotional bill-backs, and compliance fines grows exponentially.

- **Accuracy Issues:** Not all deductions are valid, some are errors or overcharges that you have the right to dispute.

- **Cash Flow Impact:** Even small percentages (2–3%) add up quickly. On $1M in sales, $20K–$30K in deductions can make or break your profitability.

- **Operational Strain:** Tracking deductions across multiple retailers, distributors, and promotional programs requires detail-oriented systems and often dedicated staff.

Common Challenges

Retailer Complexity: Each retailer has different rules, systems, and dispute processes.

. . .

Data Gaps: Without strong systems (EDI, ERP, or accounting software), it's hard to track deductions against actual sales and promotions.

Time Burden: Disputes require documentation (POs, proof of delivery, emails). Without organization, it's nearly impossible to recover funds.

Cumulative Effect: Small deductions that seem harmless add up over time and erode your bottom line.

Solutions for Managing Deductions

Dedicated Staff or Consultants

- Many growing brands hire a deduction analyst or AR specialist to track and dispute deductions.
- This role often pays for itself by recovering funds that would otherwise be lost.

Accounting and ERP Tools

- Systems like QuickBooks with add-ons, NetSuite, or SAP can help track invoices and deductions systematically.
- Specialty tools like TradeSpend360 or Crisp are designed for CPG deduction management.

Dispute Process

- Establish a straightforward workflow: log every deduction, cross-check against agreements, and dispute within the retailer's window (often 30–90 days).
- Keep all supporting documents (POs, BOLs, invoices, promotional agreements) organized in one place.

Prevention Through Compliance

- Many deductions (late deliveries, mislabeled pallets, incorrect case packs) can be prevented by strict adherence to routing guides and retailer requirements.
- Train your operations team to treat compliance as non-negotiable.

Never underestimate deductions. They're are a hidden cost of retail that can cripple an unprepared brand. Build systems for deduction management early, even if it's just a spreadsheet and filing system at first. As your business grows, be prepared to invest in software and staff.

Pro Tip: Treat deductions like a second P&L. Track them by type (spoils, chargebacks, promotions, errors), monitor trends, and calculate your "true net." This transparency will make you a stronger negotiator with buyers and distributors, and protect your profitability.

BONUS - Grocery Pricing Structures

Retail pricing isn't random, every retailer follows a structured pricing strategy that influences how products are positioned, promoted, and perceived by consumers. As a founder, understanding these pricing models helps you anticipate how your product will be priced in-store and how often it may be promoted. The two most common pricing structures are Everyday Low Price (EDLP) and High-Low.

Everyday Low Price (EDLP)

What It Is:

A pricing strategy where retailers offer consistently low prices on products rather than relying heavily on promotions or temporary discounts. Walmart is the most famous example of this model.

How It Works:

- Products are priced competitively every day.

- Retailers communicate trust to consumers: "You don't need to wait for a sale."

- Promotions are less frequent, but prices remain stable and reliable.

Implications for Founders:

- Your product must be priced sharply from the start to fit into EDLP.

- Margins may be tighter because there's less room for inflated list prices.

- Trade spend budgets are often lower with EDLP retailers, but cost efficiencies are expected.

Pro Tip: EDLP works best for products with broad appeal and high velocity. If your price point is premium, it may not align well with EDLP retailers.

High-Low

What It Is:
A pricing strategy where products are sold at a higher regular price but are frequently discounted through promotions (weekly circulars, coupons, loyalty programs). Most traditional grocery stores operate on this model.

How It Works:

- The "regular" price is higher than EDLP pricing.

- Sales and promotions temporarily lower the price to drive trial and volume.

- Shoppers are trained to "wait for the deal," promotions are a core part of the shopping experience.

Implications for Founders:

- You'll need to budget for regular promotional activity (TPRs, scan downs, loyalty discounts).

- Buyers expect a clear promotional calendar with multiple events per year.

- The higher base price can make your product appear premium, but heavy discounting is part of the game.

Pro Tip: High-Low works well for new brands looking to drive trial, promotions create urgency and visibility. Just make sure you've budgeted for the discounts.

Key Takeaway

Both pricing models affect your retail economics, promotional strategy, and brand positioning. EDLP offers stability but demands sharp pricing. High-Low allows premium positioning and trial-driving promotions but requires ongoing trade spend.

· · ·

Pro Tip: Before pitching to a retailer, study their pricing strategy. If you know they're EDLP, emphasize efficiency and competitive pricing. If they're High-Low, come prepared with a robust promotional calendar.

Freefills

Freefills are one of the earliest and most eye-opening financial realities founders encounter when entering retail. While the term itself sounds harmless, freefills can have a meaningful impact on both margins and cash flow if they're not planned for properly. In simple terms, a freefill means you are giving product away to earn your initial placement, and that cost is entirely yours to absorb.

A freefill occurs when a retailer requires you to provide a set number of cases per store at no charge in order to stock your product for the first time. These cases are used to fill the shelf at launch, ensuring the retailer can merchandise the product immediately without any upfront inventory risk. Freefills are typically required on a per-store, per-SKU basis. For example, if a chain asks for two free cases per SKU and you're launching three SKUs into 100 stores, you would be responsible for producing, packing, and shipping 600 cases with no revenue attached. You still pay for ingredients, packaging, labor, and freight, but the retailer pays nothing for those initial units.

Retailers require freefills to reduce their risk when onboarding new brands. By receiving product at no cost, they can test how well it sells without tying up their own inventory dollars. Freefills also ensure shelves are stocked from day one, which improves the shopper experience and gives consumers an immediate opportunity to discover the product. From the retailer's perspective, it's a low-risk way to evaluate whether your product earns a reorder.

For founders, the implications are significant. Freefills function as a promotional investment, similar to demos or temporary price reductions, and should be treated that way in your financial planning. If they're not budgeted for, they can quickly strain cash flow, especially during multi-store rollouts. Freefills also come with performance pressure. Because the initial inventory is free, retailers expect it to move. If sell-through is slow and shelves sit full, buyers may hesitate to reorder, making the freefill a sunk cost rather than a bridge to ongoing sales. In some cases, freefill requirements can be negotiated down, for example from three cases per store to one, but many retailers view them as non-negotiable. The key is understanding the true cost upfront and deciding whether the opportunity aligns with your financial capacity and launch readiness.

Pro Tip: Before saying yes to a new account, carefully calculate your freefill cost. Even if it feels like a huge win to be listed in hundreds of stores, the freefill burden can overwhelm your production capacity and cash reserves.

Real-World Simulation

A startup snack company secured placement in 250 regional grocery stores with 4 SKUs. The retailer required 2 free cases per SKU per store:

Total Free Cases = S x SKU x C

S = Number of Stores (250)
SKU = Number of SKUs per Store (4)
C = Free Cases Required per SKU per Store (2)

Total Free Cases = 250 Stores x 4 SKUs x 2 cases
Total Free Cases = 2,000 cases

At a production cost of $15 per case, the freefill represented a $30,000 upfront expense, before a single dollar of revenue came in.

Pro Tip: Treat freefills like marketing spend, not sales. They are an investment in shelf presence, trial, and long-term growth. If your margins are thin or your cash is limited, focus on smaller rollouts where the freefill burden is manageable.

Your Product Promotions Calendar

Promotions drive trial, visibility, and repeat purchases, but only if they're executed with precision. A promotions calendar ensures your team, distributor, and retailer partners are all aligned on *what's being promoted, when, and where.* Without a calendar, promotions risk becoming reactive, scattered, and ineffective.

A well-structured calendar serves two key purposes:

Internal Alignment: Your marketing and sales teams know what SKUs are on deal at any given time, so they can plan advertising, digital campaigns, and influencer activations accordingly.

Retailer Alignment: Retailers expect manufacturers to plan promotions in advance and commit to them, often on a quarterly or annual basis. Your calendar becomes a tool to demonstrate professionalism and reliability.

Universal Calendar (SKU and Season Specific)

The universal calendar is built around your brand's priorities and seasonality. It ensures your team has a roadmap for spotlighting specific SKUs at the right times.

Examples:

- **BBQ Sauces:** Featured in May–July for grilling season.

- **Pumpkin or Spiced SKUs:** Promoted heavily in September–November.

- **Better-for-You Snacks:** Tied to January "New Year, New You" campaigns.

Why It Matters:

- Keeps consumer marketing consistent across retail and DTC channels.

- Maximizes consumer resonance by aligning promotions with natural purchase cycles.

- Provides clear direction for your internal team and external partners (PR, digital agencies, etc.).

Pro Tip: Build your universal calendar at least 6–12 months in advance. It will serve as your *north star* when planning marketing campaigns and allocating trade spend.

Store Specific Calendar

This calendar is developed in partnership with retail customers. Every major retailer operates with its own promotional schedule, sometimes quarterly, sometimes tied to seasonal themes, and always negotiated in advance.

Examples:

- A national chain might require you to participate in Back-to-School promos in August and Holiday promos in December.

- Regional grocers may offer monthly circulars or loyalty program spotlights.

- Promotions can be channel-specific, such as drug channel discounts in January (wellness season) or club pack promotions during summer travel season.

Why It Matters:

- Ensures you stay compliant with retailer agreements.

- Builds trust and reliability with buyers (they know you'll show up when planned).

- Helps you coordinate inventory, production, and logistics to support spikes in demand.

Pro Tip: Never promise promotions you can't deliver. Missing a committed promo window damages retailer trust and risks future shelf space.

Key Takeaway

A promotions calendar is an essential tool that ties together marketing, sales, operations, and retail partnerships. Done right, it ensures your brand shows up consistently, consumers see you when they're ready to buy, and your retailer partners view you as a dependable, professional supplier.

Pro Tip: Use simple tools (Excel, Google Sheets, or a shared calendar system) to manage promotions at first. As you grow, upgrade to trade promotion management (TPM) software to track spend, ROI, and execution across all accounts.

Plan-o-Gram

Once your product is accepted by a retailer, one of the most important and least discussed documents you'll encounter is the plan-o-gram, often called a POG. A plan-o-gram dictates exactly where and how your product appears on the shelf, and it plays a major role in visibility, compliance, and sales performance. For founders, understanding how plan-o-grams work helps explain why some products fly off the shelf while others struggle, even within the same category.

A plan-o-gram is a visual schematic created by a retailer's merchandising or category team that shows the layout of an entire category. It specifies where each product sits, how many facings it receives, and at what shelf height it's placed. These layouts are designed to maximize category sales, profitability, and the overall shopper experience by carefully balancing brands, sizes, price points, and consumer buying patterns. In larger retailers, plan-o-grams are often data-driven and may be influenced by category captains, typically large manufacturers that help analyze trends and performance within the category.

Plan-o-grams matter because shelf placement directly affects sales. Products placed at eye level or on endcaps consistently outperform those on top or bottom shelves. The number of facings your product receives also has a measurable impact on velocity. A single facing limits visibility, while two or three facings can significantly increase trial simply by making the product easier to see and grab. From the retailer's perspective, plan-o-grams are strategic tools, not aesthetic choices. They reflect what the data suggests will sell best and deliver the strongest return per square foot.

Retailers also expect strict compliance with plan-o-grams. Shelves should be stocked exactly as specified, whether that responsibility falls to store staff, distributors, or merchandisers. Failure to comply can result in penalties, reduced support, or even loss of placement. For founders, it's important to know that you typically have limited control over initial plan-o-gram decisions, especially as a new brand. However, that control can be earned over time. Strong velocity, consistent in-stock performance, and clear proof of consumer demand are the most effective ways to influence future resets.

Plan-o-grams are usually updated on a set schedule, often once or twice a year. These reset periods are critical moments when new products are added, underperforming items are removed, and shelf space is reallocated. For founders, this means timing matters. If your product is performing well when resets occur, you have a better chance of gaining additional facings or improved placement. In the end, data wins. Consistently tracking and sharing performance metrics is the most reliable path to earning better shelf real estate and long-term retail success.

Real-World Simulation

Trail, a premium granola brand, initially launched in a regional chain with one facing on the bottom shelf. After six months of strong velocities (20+ UPSPW), the buyer added two additional flavors and gave them two facings of each SKU at eye level. Sales doubled almost immediately, proving that placement is just as important as distribution.

Figure: Plan-o-gram

When pitching buyers, ask:

- *"Where would my product be positioned on the shelf?"*

- *"How many facings can we start with?"*

- *"When is your next category reset?"*

This shows you understand the mechanics of retail and positions you as a serious partner.

Pro Tip: Regularly take photos of your product in-store. Compare actual placement to the plan-o-gram. If there are compliance issues (your product is missing, misplaced, or out of stock), work with your distributor or retailer rep to fix them immediately.

BONUS - PLAN-O-GRAM OPTIMIZATION STRATEGIES

While early-stage brands rarely control plan-o-grams outright, they can absolutely influence placement over time. Retailers are pragmatic, they reward what works. The single most powerful lever you have is velocity. When your product consistently outperforms category averages, you give buyers a clear, data-backed reason to allocate more space. Shelves exist to turn, and strong sell-through is often what moves a brand from a single facing on a lower shelf to multiple facings at eye level during the next reset.

Founders should also learn to advocate for facings, not assume they'll be granted automatically. Facings are a negotiation point, especially when tied to trade support. If you're committing to demos, temporary price reductions, or retailer advertising, it's reasonable to ask for additional facings in return. Promotions can also influence placement beyond the main shelf. Retailers often award secondary placements, such as end caps, shippers, or side stacks, to brands funding compelling promotions. A well-timed offer, like a back-to-school BOGO, can earn premium visibility even for a young brand.

Placement arguments are strongest when framed around shopper logic rather than brand preference. If your product performs better next to complementary items or serves a specific shopper mission, make that case clearly. Buyers are often receptive to insights that improve the shopping experience and basket size. Finally, don't overlook the human side of execution. Plan-o-gram compliance isn't always perfect at the store level, and relationships matter. Store managers, stockers, distributor reps, and broker teams play a critical role in how shelves actually look. Strong relationships with these partners can help ensure correct placement, faster corrections, and, over time, better positioning for your brand.

Pro Tip: Aim for Secondary Placements. Beyond the plan-o-gram'ed shelf, look for:

- **End Caps** (high-visibility displays at aisle ends)
- **Shippers** (freestanding cardboard displays)
- **Checkout Lanes** (impulse placement)

These often require extra promotional spend but deliver strong visibility.

Resets

One of the most consequential and often nerve-wracking moments in grocery retail is the reset. Resets are scheduled events when retailers reorganize shelves, update assortments, and physically re-merchandise entire categories based on new plan-o-grams. For brands, a reset represents a clear inflection point. It can open the door to new placement, additional facings, or better visibility, or it can result in reduced space or complete discontinuation if performance hasn't met expectations.

Resets matter because they are the primary gateway for new products. Most retailers only add or remove items during these periods, which means missing a reset can delay growth by months. They also reflect broader category strategy shifts. As consumer preferences evolve, resets are used to expand fast-growing segments and trim underperforming ones. Placement decisions made during a reset, whether eye level, bottom shelf, or secondary displays, can significantly influence velocity. Just as importantly, resets are when buyers formally evaluate performance. Sales data, fill rates, and promotional support are reviewed, and products that don't justify their space are often cut.

The reset process typically begins months in advance, with

retailers communicating reset calendars and submission timelines. Category managers determine which products stay, which exit, and which new items are added. Merchandising teams then develop updated plan-o-grams, often informed by category captains or syndicated data. Execution happens in-store, carried out by store staff, distributor reps, or third-party reset teams, with brands expected to comply exactly with the new layout.

For founders, navigating resets successfully requires preparation and vigilance. Always ask buyers about reset timing and build your sales and production forecasts around it. Bring data to the table, strong velocity, consumer demand, and proof of trade support are your best defenses. After a reset, visit stores to ensure your product is placed correctly and fully faced, as execution errors are common. Stay flexible and work closely with distributors or brokers to monitor compliance and correct issues quickly. Finally, plan for short-term disruption. Orders may temporarily dip as shelves are reworked, so resets should be anticipated in both cash flow and inventory planning.

Real-World Simulation

A frozen entrée brand struggled with bottom-shelf placement during its first year. At the annual reset, the buyer expanded the brand into the plant-based frozen section (a growing subcategory) and gave them two additional facings. Sales jumped by 50% within two months.

Pro Tip: Think of resets as both a risk and an opportunity. If your performance is strong, resets can be your moment to expand. If not, they may be when you're cut. Plan ahead, bring your best data, and always align with your buyer before reset season.

Shelf Placement

Not all shelf space is created equal, and where your product lives in a store has a direct impact on how often it's seen and how quickly it sells. Shelf placement generally falls into two categories: primary placement, which is your product's permanent home within its category, and secondary placement, which places your product elsewhere in the store for added visibility. Both play important but distinct roles in driving awareness, trial, and repeat purchase.

Primary placement is your product's core location within its assigned category, such as granola in the cereal aisle or salsa in condiments. This is where shoppers expect to find you, and it's where buyers evaluate your performance most closely. Velocity benchmarks, category comparisons, and long-term decisions about whether you stay on shelf are all tied to how you perform in this set. For founders, this is the make-or-break placement. Secondary displays can provide a lift, but they rarely compensate for weak performance in your primary location.

Primary Placement (In Category Set)

What It Is:
The standard location for your product within its assigned category (ex., granola in the cereal aisle, salsa in the condiments aisle, yogurt in dairy).

Why It Matters:

- This is where consumers expect to find your product.

- Buyers evaluate your performance primarily based on sales in this location.

- Velocity benchmarks are tied to primary placement.

Founder Tip: Your success or failure as a brand is judged most directly by your performance in primary placement. Secondary placements are a bonus, but they rarely save a brand that can't perform in its set.

Figure: Primary Placement

Secondary placement refers to additional, out-of-category locations designed to increase visibility and encourage impulse or cross-category purchases. Examples include placing salsa near salty snacks, single-serve hummus and pretzel packs near the salad bar, or energy bars at checkout. These placements matter because they expose your product to shoppers who might not otherwise encounter it, often leading to incremental sales. They also signal retailer confidence, as secondary placement is typically reserved for brands the retailer wants to actively promote. However, access is limited, costs are higher, and placements are usually temporary or seasonal, often tied to promotions, free fills, or additional trade spend.

Secondary Placement (Out of Category)

What It Is:
Additional placements in high-visibility or complementary areas of the store. These are *coveted opportunities* that can dramatically boost trial.

Why It Matters:

- **Visibility:** Shoppers may not walk down every aisle, but secondary placement increases your chances of being seen.

- **Incremental Sales:** Encourages impulse purchases and cross-category trial.

- **Retailer Support:** Secondary placement is a strong signal that the retailer believes in your brand and wants to drive sales.

Challenges with Secondary Placement

- **Limited Access:** Often reserved for category leaders or brands investing heavily in promotions.

- **Costly:** May require additional promotional spend, free cases, or slotting fees.

- **Temporary:** Many secondary placements are promotional or seasonal, not permanent.

Figure: Secondary Placement

Within primary placement, vertical shelf positioning plays a major role in visibility and sales. As we'll discuss in the next chapter, high-level placement, on the top shelf, tends to be less effective for new brands, as shoppers are less likely to look up unless they're specifically searching. Eye-level placement, often called "buy level," is the most valuable real estate on the shelf. Products here benefit from maximum visibility and ease of grab, and as a result, see the strongest sales performance. Retailers typically reserve these positions for proven performers, high-margin items, or brands investing heavily in promotions. Bottom-shelf placement is where many startups begin. While visibility is lower, especially for adult shoppers, strong packaging and promotions can still drive trial, and many successful brands have worked their way up over time by proving velocity.

A common real-world scenario illustrates the power of placement. A tortilla chip startup launched with modest sales in the salty snacks aisle. During football season, the retailer added a secondary end-cap alongside salsa and guacamole. Weekly sales tripled during the promotion, reinforcing how placement, not just product quality, drives performance. For founders, the takeaway is clear: always ask about placement when planning promotions. Framing the request as a partnership, investing in a TPR or demos in exchange for secondary placement, aligns your goals with the retailer's and increases the likelihood of success.

Pro Tip: Always ask buyers about secondary placement opportunities when planning promotions. Position it as mutually beneficial: "If we're investing in a TPR and demos, can we also get a secondary display in produce or deli?" Retailers want promotions to succeed, and requests framed around stronger sell-through are usually received more favorably than requests framed around visibility alone.

Shelf Positioning

Shelf positioning plays a meaningful role in how shoppers encounter and ultimately choose products. Not all shelf space is created equal, and where your product sits within a set can significantly influence visibility, trial, and velocity.

High Level

Products placed on the top shelf, typically above eye level, are often reserved for specialty items, oversized packaging, or products that are purchased less frequently. While this placement may make sense from a merchandising perspective, it can reduce visibility, as most shoppers do not naturally look upward unless they are actively searching for a specific item. In certain categories with highly intentional consumers, such as gluten-free or specialty baking, top-shelf placement can still perform if shoppers are motivated and know what they are looking for. For emerging brands, however, this is generally the least favorable position and often requires additional promotional support or signage to drive awareness and trial.

Shelf Positioning

High Level

What It Is:
The top shelf of a set, usually above eye level for most shoppers.

Implications:

- Typically reserved for specialty, oversized, or less frequently purchased products.

- Can reduce visibility since shoppers rarely look up unless they're actively searching.

- Works better for categories with loyal, destination-driven shoppers (ex., gluten-free flour buyers will search the top shelf if they know what they want).

Founder Tip: High-level positioning is usually the least favorable for new brands. If placed here, you'll need strong promotional support and signage to drive trial.

Figure: High Level

Eye Level

Eye level placement, often referred to as "buy level," represents the most valuable real estate on the shelf. These shelves align directly with a shopper's natural line of sight, making products easier to notice and pick up without effort. As a result, items placed at eye level tend to experience the highest sales lift. Retailers typically reserve this space for category leaders, high-performing products, or brands that contribute significant margin or promotional investment. For newer brands, securing this position early is uncommon. A more realistic approach is to demonstrate strong performance in lower placements and use that data to negotiate improved positioning during future category reviews or resets.

Shelf Positioning

Eye Level ("Buy Level")

What It Is:
The shelves aligned directly with a shopper's line of sight, typically 4–5 feet off the ground.

Implications:

- The most valuable real estate on the shelf.

- Products here see the highest sales lift due to visibility and ease of grab.

- Retailers usually reserve eye-level placement for category leaders, high-margin products, or brands paying higher slotting or promotional fees.

Founder Tip: If you can't secure eye-level placement initially, prove velocity at lower levels. Strong performance gives you leverage to negotiate better positioning during resets.

Figure: Eye Level

Low Level

The bottom shelf, positioned near the floor, generally offers the lowest visibility and convenience for shoppers. Because most consumers naturally scan shelves from eye level downward, products placed at the lowest level are easier to overlook, particularly in crowded categories with many competing items. Shoppers may also be less inclined to bend down unless they are specifically searching for a product or comparing prices closely.

For emerging brands, bottom-shelf placement is a common starting point, especially in highly competitive categories where premium shelf real estate is reserved for established brands or high-performing SKUs. While this placement can create visibility challenges, success is still possible with strong packaging, clear branding, and strategic shopper marketing support. Shelf talkers, promotions, and secondary displays can help draw attention and encourage shoppers to engage with products that may otherwise fall outside their natural line of sight.

Shelf Positioning

Low Level

What It Is:
Shelf placement located closest to the floor, typically offering the lowest visibility within the set for adult shoppers.

Implications:

- Lower natural visibility compared to eye- and hand-level placement
- Reduced impulse discovery and shopper engagement
- May require shoppers to bend down or search intentionally
- Often used for emerging brands, lower-velocity SKUs, or value-oriented products

Founder Tip:
If your product is placed on a lower shelf, focus on bold packaging, strong color blocking, and shopper marketing tools like shelf talkers or secondary displays to help draw attention and improve visibility.

Figure: Low Level

Shelf positioning is a critical factor in retail performance. A product placed at eye level can outsell the same item on the bottom shelf by a significant margin. While founders may not always control where their product is placed, they are responsible for understanding that placement, supporting it with strong in-store and marketing efforts, and using performance data to improve their position over time.

FACINGS

In grocery retail, *facings* refer to how many units of your product appear side by side on the shelf. Facings aren't just about physical space, they directly influence visibility, shopper perception, and sales velocity. More facings make your product easier to spot, signal importance to shoppers, and reduce the likelihood of an empty-looking shelf. For founders, facings are one of the most powerful yet underestimated drivers of performance at retail.

A single facing is the most common starting point for new or small brands. With only one unit visible, your product competes against established brands that often have multiple facings and far greater shelf presence. Single facings also increase the risk of out-of-stocks, as just a few purchases can wipe out your visible inventory. When this is your reality, packaging, clear branding, and promotional activity matter even more, they must work harder to pull the shopper's eye.

Double facings place two units next to each other and can meaningfully change how a product performs. Two facings make your brand feel more substantial and easier to notice, while also giving you a buffer against empty shelves. Retailers often view double facings as something to be earned, either through strong velocity or additional trade support. In practice, adding a second facing can dramatically increase sales, not because demand suddenly changes, but because visibility does.

At the other end of the spectrum are brand blocks, sometimes called the "billboard effect." Large manufacturers dominate entire sections of shelf space with multiple SKUs grouped together, creating an unmistakable visual presence. Think of Oreo filling several feet of the cookie aisle or Coca-Cola controlling entire cooler doors. These blocks draw the shopper's eye instantly and reinforce brand leadership and trust. While smaller brands can't compete at that scale, grouping two or three SKUs together can still create a powerful micro-billboard effect that improves recognition and shopability.

The key takeaway for founders is that facings are sales multipliers. Each incremental facing increases visibility, credibility, and the likelihood of purchase. Earning more facings requires proof, strong velocity, effective promotions, and trust with the retailer. Over time, consistent performance turns a single facing into multiple facings, and multiple facings into a meaningful presence.

A final practical note: always check your facings during store visits. Extra facings have a way of disappearing as shelves get condensed or reset. Distributor and broker reps can be valuable allies here, helping ensure plan-o-gram compliance and protecting the shelf space you've worked hard to earn.

Typical Logistics Contractual Terms and Conditions

When working with carriers, 3PLs, distributors, or freight forwarders, you'll encounter standard terms and conditions (T&Cs) that define how goods are handled, shipped, and delivered. Founders often overlook these details, but they can have a direct impact on costs, liability, and customer relationships. Understanding these terms protects your brand from costly mistakes.

Common Terms and Conditions to Expect

Delivery Windows and Appointment Scheduling

- Retailers and distributors often require strict delivery appointments.
- Missed or late appointments may result in chargebacks or refused deliveries.

Freight Prepaid vs. Freight Collect

- **Freight Prepaid:** Shipper (you) pays freight charges upfront.

- **Freight Collect:** Receiver pays upon delivery.

Most startups ship prepaid until they have leverage to negotiate otherwise.

Incoterms (FOB, CIF, etc.)

- Define who is responsible for costs and risk at each stage of the shipping journey.

Example: FOB (Free on Board) means the buyer assumes responsibility once the goods leave your dock.

Minimum Order Quantities (MOQs)

- Logistics partners and distributors may set minimum shipment volumes.
- Failing to meet them could result in surcharges or delayed shipments.

Payment Terms

- Freight invoices are typically due in 30 days (Net 30).
- Distributors may stretch to 45–60 days or longer. Plan cash flow accordingly.

Claims and Liability

- Who is responsible if goods arrive damaged, spoiled, or short?
- Typically: Carrier liability is limited by weight (ex., $0.50/lb.), unless you purchase additional insurance.
- Always document damage with photos and note issues on the Bill of Lading.

Accessorial Charges

- Carriers may tack on extra fees (liftgate, detention, residential delivery).
- These are spelled out in T&Cs but often missed by founders until invoices arrive.

Pallet Standards and Packaging Requirements

- Most retailers require 40x48-inch pallets, shrink-wrapped and labeled.
- Failure to follow spec sheets can result in fines or refused deliveries.

Temperature Requirements

- For cold chain products, maintaining temperature is mandatory at every stage.
- T&Cs will define acceptable ranges and who bears responsibility if temps drift.

Routing Guides

- Large retailers issue routing guides, detailed instructions for labeling, pallet configuration, and delivery windows.
- Not following them = chargebacks, fines, or delayed payments.

Why It Matters for Founders

- **Hidden Costs:** Many logistics costs don't show up until you read the fine print.

- **Liability:** Knowing who bears responsibility for damaged goods can save thousands.

- **Credibility:** Buyers expect founders to understand T&Cs; ignorance looks unprofessional.

- **Negotiation:** As your volumes grow, you'll gain leverage to negotiate more favorable terms.

Pro Tip: Always review logistics contracts with a lawyer or consultant before signing. A small upfront investment in clarity can prevent much larger losses down the road.

BONUS - Direct-to-Consumer (DTC) for Product Validation

Before jumping into retail distribution, many founders start by selling directly to consumers. DTC not only generates early revenue but also provides real-world feedback on your product, branding, and pricing. It's one of the most effective ways to validate whether your product resonates before investing heavily in retail channels.

The key benefit of DTC validation is that you can test and iterate quickly, adjusting packaging, messaging, and even formulations based on what customers tell you face-to-face.

Farmers Markets

Why They Work:
Farmers markets are one of the lowest-barrier entry points for food entrepreneurs. They allow you to present your product to a community audience, test pricing, and gather honest consumer reactions.

Benefits:

- Immediate feedback on taste, packaging, and pricing.

- Affordable booth fees ($50–$200 per market day).

- Direct cash flow without distributor or retailer margins.

- Storytelling opportunity, customers love meeting founders.

Founder Tips:

- Always sample, shoppers are more likely to buy once they taste.

- Pay attention to repeat buyers; they validate product-market fit.

- Use simple feedback prompts ("What made you buy?" / "What would you change?").

- Track sales volume by week to see if momentum builds.

Pop-Up Shops

Why They Work:

Pop-ups are temporary retail activations in high-traffic locations like shopping centers, shared kitchens, or partner retail spaces. They let you test brand positioning in a more retail-like setting.

Benefits:

- Exposure to new customers beyond farmers market audiences.

- Opportunities to test merchandising and point-of-sale displays.

- Partnerships with other brands or spaces can reduce costs.

- Potential for local press and social buzz.

Founder Tips:

- Keep branding simple but professional, a strong table set up goes a long way.

- Use QR codes for instant sign-ups to your email list or online store.

- Consider themed pop-ups (holidays, local festivals) for higher foot traffic.

- Collect feedback not only on product but also on how shoppers interact with your display.

OTHER OPPORTUNITIES FOR PRODUCT VALIDATION

In-Kind Sponsorships

Why They Work:

Providing free product in exchange for visibility at community or industry events is an effective low-cost way to get trial. Unlike paid advertising, this approach ensures real people taste your product, and often in a context that creates goodwill.

Benefits:

- Cost-effective exposure to hundreds of potential consumers.

- Aligns your brand with causes, organizations, or events your target market values.

- Generates sampling data ("How many people tried it? How many wanted more?").

- Potential to create word-of-mouth buzz.

Founder Tips:

- Choose sponsorships wisely, align with events that attract your target consumer.

- Make sure your logo and story are visible alongside your samples.

- Gather feedback onsite if possible (quick surveys, QR codes for follow-up).

- Don't overextend; in-kind should be strategic, not endless free product.

Our Founders' Journey

Elena - Harbor Harvest Foods
(Spiced Mango Preserves)

After a successful run at local farmers markets, Elena finally approached a small neighborhood grocer about carrying *Harbor Harvest Foods*. The buyer loved her preserves but asked questions she hadn't anticipated, case counts, UPCs, shelf life, and delivery schedule. She left the meeting humbled but determined. Within a month, she had barcodes ordered, packaging adjusted, and her first retail placement confirmed. The day she saw her jars on shelf, she realized: distribution is equal parts delivery and discipline.

Marcus - Summit Sips (Clean
Labeled Sparkling Iced Tea)

Marcus secured regional distribution and celebrated the milestone, until his first invoice arrived with unexpected deductions. It wasn't failure; it was education. He started paying closer attention to his *freight costs, slotting fees, and distributor allowances*, recognizing that growth meant new layers of complexity. Still, by building relationships with his distributor's sales reps and staying visible at store level, he learned how to keep *Summit Sips* moving instead of just shipping.

Danielle - Bountiful Bites (Upcycled Snacks)

Fueled by her early retail wins, Danielle said "yes" to every opportunity, from independent stores to regional chains. Within months, she was juggling multiple distributors and struggling to keep up with purchase orders. Deliveries ran late, deductions piled up, and communication broke down. Her enthusiasm outpaced her infrastructure. For the first time, she understood that scaling isn't about saying yes to every opportunity, it's about saying yes *strategically*.

Andre - Kindred Grains
(Ancient Grain Snacks)

Andre took a methodical approach, partnering with a local distributor for *Kindred Grains* while still selling direct to key independent accounts. By maintaining a hybrid model, he kept his margins healthy and his relationships strong. When a national retailer approached him, he didn't rush. Instead, he asked for their *category review timeline* and aligned his next production cycle accordingly. He had learned that in distribution, timing was everything, and patience was a competitive advantage.

CHAPTER TWO

Promotions (Marketing)

For many food founders, marketing is assumed to be nothing more than social media or advertising. Others believe that a great product will naturally "market itself." In reality, marketing is much broader and far more strategic.

At its core, marketing is the process of creating awareness, shaping perception, and influencing behavior. It is how consumers discover your product, understand its value, remember your brand, and ultimately decide to purchase it.

In CPG, marketing is especially important because shoppers are making decisions quickly and with limited attention. Your product is competing not only against direct competitors, but against every other item fighting for visibility in the store, online, and in the consumer's mind.

This chapter serves as a practical foundation for founders who may not come from a marketing background. The goal is not to turn you into a marketing expert overnight, but to help you understand the core principles that drive brand growth in the food industry.

The Importance of Positioning

Before a promotion, advertisement, or social post can be effective, you must first understand your positioning. Positioning is the space your product occupies in the consumer's mind relative to competitors.

It answers questions such as:

- What makes this product different?
- Who is it for?
- Why should someone choose it?
- Is it value-oriented, premium, functional, indulgent, sustainable, or convenience-driven?

Strong positioning creates clarity. Weak positioning creates confusion. Your packaging, pricing, messaging, ingredients, and promotions should all reinforce the same positioning. If your product claims to be premium but is constantly discounted, shoppers may question its value. If your messaging changes constantly, consumers may struggle to understand what your brand stands for.

Understanding Your Target Consumer

One of the biggest mistakes founders make is trying to market to everyone. Effective marketing begins with understanding your ideal consumer.

This includes:

- Demographics (age, income, family structure)
- Lifestyle and values
- Shopping habits
- Health and dietary preferences
- Price sensitivity
- Purchase motivations

The more clearly you understand your target consumer, the easier it becomes to create messaging, packaging, and promotions that resonate.

Marketing is most effective when consumers feel like the product was created specifically for them.

Awareness vs. Conversion

Not all marketing serves the same purpose. Some efforts are designed to build awareness, while others are designed to drive immediate purchase.

Awareness Marketing focuses on introducing the brand and building familiarity. Examples include:

- Social media content
- Public relations
- Influencer partnerships
- Podcasts
- Experiential events

These activities help consumers recognize and remember your brand.

Conversion Marketing focuses on driving action. Examples include:

- Coupons
- Digital ads with direct purchase links
- Sampling programs
- Temporary price reductions
- Retail media ads
- Affiliate programs

These tactics encourage consumers to purchase now rather than later. Healthy brands typically need both. Awareness creates interest. Conversion turns interest into sales.

The Consumer Journey

The path to purchase is often described as a journey because consumers move through stages before becoming loyal buyers. The key stages are:

1. **Awareness** → "I recognize this brand or product exists."
2. **Relevance** → "This product feels aligned with my needs, lifestyle, values, or preferences."
3. **Acceptance** → "I'm willing to try or purchase this product."
4. **Preference** → "I prefer this product over competing options, and I actively seek out, recommend, and consistently return to this brand."

Many founders focus heavily on awareness while underinvesting in repeat purchase. In CPG, repeat purchase is critical because long-term growth depends on consumers returning to the product consistently.

Brand Marketing vs. Product Marketing

While often grouped together, brand marketing and product marketing are not exactly the same.

Brand Marketing focuses on the larger identity and emotional connection behind the company. It shapes perception and builds long-term equity.
Examples include:

- Brand story
- Visual identity
- Mission and values
- Lifestyle positioning

Product Marketing focuses more directly on the item itself and why someone should buy it.
Examples include:

- Flavor launches
- Functional benefits
- Pricing and promotions
- Product demonstrations

Strong brands align both so the product and the broader brand identity reinforce each other.

The Importance of Consistency

Consistency is one of the most underrated principles in marketing. Consumers trust brands that feel stable and recognizable.

This includes consistency across:

- Packaging
- Tone of voice
- Visual identity
- Messaging
- Promotional strategy

Frequent shifts in design or communication can confuse consumers and weaken recognition over time.

Measuring Marketing Effectiveness

Marketing should not operate entirely on intuition. Founders should track performance whenever possible.

Common metrics include:

- Sales lift
- Repeat purchase behavior
- Coupon redemption
- Website traffic
- Social engagement
- Email sign-ups
- Return on ad spend (ROAS)

Measurement helps founders understand what is working, what is underperforming, and where future investment should go.

Marketing is a key business strategy, one of the primary ways your brand and product become visible to the world.

In CPG, great products alone are rarely enough. Consumers must notice the product, understand it, trust it, and remember it. Effective marketing creates that connection.

For founders, the goal is to understand the principles behind how brands grow, communicate clearly, and consistently create reasons for consumers to choose them again and again.

The Difference Between Trade, Shopper, and Consumer Marketing

Understanding the distinction between trade marketing, shopper marketing, and consumer marketing is one of the most important mindset shifts for founders entering retail. While these areas often work together and may even share budget dollars, they are designed for different audiences and serve different strategic purposes. Confusing them can lead to misplaced investment, unrealistic expectations, and weak execution across the business.

Trade Marketing

Trade marketing is directed toward the gatekeepers of distribution, retailers, distributors, brokers, and category managers. Its purpose is to secure placement, strengthen retail relationships, and support the business case for carrying your product. Trade marketing focuses on convincing the trade that your brand deserves shelf space, promotional support, and long-term investment.

These efforts may include slotting fees, off-invoice discounts, distributor programs, trade advertising, trade shows, retailer presentations, and other investments tied to placement and retail partnership development. The goal is not immediate consumer demand. The goal is gaining access to the shelf and reinforcing your credibility as a supplier.

Shopper Marketing

Shopper marketing sits between the trade and the consumer. It focuses on influencing behavior at or near the point of purchase, whether inside the store or through retailer-connected digital channels. Shopper marketing is designed to convert presence into purchase by guiding the shopper toward your product at the moment decisions are being made.

This includes tools such as shelf talkers, floor displays, end caps, circulars, retailer apps, loyalty programs, in-store signage, digital coupons, and sampling. Shopper marketing is highly tactical and closely tied to retail execution. If trade marketing gets you onto the shelf, shopper marketing helps ensure your product stands out once it is there.

Consumer Marketing

Consumer marketing, by contrast, operates more broadly and focuses on building awareness, affinity, and long-term brand equity. These are the activities consumers encounter outside of the immediate retail environment. Consumer marketing creates recognition and emotional connection so that shoppers already know, trust, or seek out your brand before entering the store.

Examples include social media campaigns, influencer partnerships, PR, experiential activations, podcasts, out-of-home advertising, brand storytelling, and broader digital marketing initiatives. While these efforts may not always drive immediate sales, they shape perception and build demand over time.

Healthy growth requires all three areas working together. Trade marketing secures access. Shopper marketing drives conversion at the shelf. Consumer marketing builds awareness and long-term brand preference. When aligned properly, they create a connected system that supports both immediate sales and sustainable growth.

Many founders overinvest in one area while neglecting the others. A brand may generate strong consumer buzz but struggle to secure distribution without trade support. Another may achieve placement but fail to move product because shopper marketing was overlooked. Others may focus heavily on retail promotions without building broader consumer awareness that supports long-term loyalty.

The strongest brands understand how these functions reinforce one another. Consumer marketing creates interest. Trade marketing creates opportunity. Shopper marketing converts intent into purchase. When these elements operate together, they create momentum that supports velocity, strengthens retailer confidence, and expands distribution over time.

Why Founders Must Balance All Three

- Trade marketing gets you onto the shelf.
- Shopper marketing gets you noticed at the shelf.
- Consumer marketing builds demand before the shopper arrives.

Without trade marketing, distribution may never happen. Without shopper marketing, products may sit unnoticed once placed. Without consumer marketing, long-term brand awareness and loyalty may never develop.

Pro Tip: Track trade, shopper, and consumer marketing separately within your budget whenever possible. Each serves a different purpose, operates on different timelines, and should be evaluated against different performance expectations. Clear tracking helps founders allocate resources more strategically and better understand which investments are truly driving growth.

The Importance of Brand and Product Promotions

One of the most common attitudes among early-stage founders is believing that once a product reaches the shelf, sales will naturally follow. In reality, retail is an intensely competitive environment where thousands of products compete for limited shopper attention every day. Even exceptional products can struggle if they are not actively supported through promotion.

Brand and product promotions are the activities used to increase visibility, encourage trial, reinforce awareness, and drive sales. They help introduce consumers to your product, create reasons to purchase, and keep your brand relevant within a crowded marketplace. In CPG, promotions are not optional extras reserved for large companies. They are a fundamental part of how products gain traction and maintain momentum.

Promotions can take many forms. Some are designed to create immediate conversion, such as coupons, demos, or temporary price reductions. Others focus on long-term awareness and brand equity, including social campaigns, PR, experiential marketing, and partnerships. While the tactics may differ, the objective remains the same: keeping your product visible and compelling to both shoppers and retail partners.

Why Promotions Matter

Retailers expect brands to support their products. Shelf placement alone does not guarantee success, and buyers closely monitor whether brands are investing in sell-through. Products that are actively promoted tend to generate stronger velocity, better shopper engagement, and increased repeat purchase, all of which strengthen retailer confidence.

Promotions also help reduce consumer hesitation. New products often face skepticism simply because shoppers are unfamiliar with them. Promotional activity creates opportunities for education, exposure, and trial, helping consumers feel more comfortable choosing your product over a familiar competitor.

For emerging brands, promotions are especially important during launch periods, retail expansion, and seasonal selling windows. These moments often determine whether a product gains momentum or quietly stalls.

Balancing Short-Term Sales and Long-Term Brand Building

Not all promotions are designed to produce immediate sales. Some investments focus on short-term conversion, while others build awareness and emotional connection over time.

Short-term promotional efforts may include:

- In-store demos and sampling
- Coupons and discounts
- Temporary price reductions
- Retail displays and end caps

Long-term brand-building efforts may include:

- Social media campaigns
- Influencer partnerships

- Public relations
- Experiential activations
- Content creation and storytelling

The strongest brands balance both. Immediate sales activity helps drive velocity and retailer confidence, while broader brand-building creates recognition and loyalty that sustain growth over time.

Strategic Promotion Planning

Effective promotions are intentional. Rather than promoting constantly, strong brands align promotions with specific objectives, such as:

- Launching a new product
- Supporting a retail expansion
- Increasing awareness in a key market
- Driving trial during seasonal periods
- Reinforcing premium positioning

Promotions should also align with inventory levels, retailer timing, and operational capacity. Poorly timed promotions can lead to stockouts, margin pressure, or wasted investment.

Measurement is equally important. Founders should evaluate promotional effectiveness through metrics such as sales lift, redemption rates, repeat purchase behavior, and return on investment. Promotions that cannot be measured are difficult to improve.

The Financial Reality of Promotions

Promotions require funding, and those costs must be planned for early. Many founders underestimate how much ongoing promotional support is required to compete effectively in retail.

These investments may include:

- Trade promotions
- Shopper marketing programs
- Sampling costs
- Digital advertising
- Retail media network spend
- Promotional discounts and allowances

Because promotions reduce net revenue in the short term, they should always be evaluated against their ability to drive long-term growth and sustainable sales performance.

In CPG, products rarely succeed because they are simply available. They succeed because consumers notice them, understand them, and feel motivated to purchase them repeatedly.

Brand and product promotions create that momentum. They transform shelf presence into shopper engagement and awareness into action. For founders, promotions are not just marketing activities, they are strategic growth tools that help turn products into lasting brands.

Our Founders' Journey

Elena - Harbor Harvest Foods (Spiced Mango Preserves)

Elena entered the business with strong intuition around storytelling, but limited formal marketing experience. Her strength came from authenticity. She naturally connected with consumers through farmers markets, in-store conversations, and social content rooted in family recipes and cultural inspiration. Over time, Elena realized that consistency mattered just as much as creativity. She began refining her messaging, improving her visual identity, and thinking more intentionally about how every touchpoint reinforced the brand. Her growth as a marketer came from learning how to translate personal passion into a repeatable and recognizable brand experience.

Marcus - Summit Sips (Clean Labeled Sparkling Iced Tea)

Marcus approached marketing from a much more structured and performance-driven perspective. Having worked around investors and growth-oriented business environments, he understood early that marketing was both a brand-building function and a financial investment. Marcus focused heavily on data, customer acquisition, and measurable return on investment. He quickly became comfortable with concepts like conversion, targeting, and promotional efficiency. However, he also learned that strong metrics alone do not create emotional connection. As the brand matured, Marcus began investing more in storytelling and lifestyle positioning to complement the analytical side of his strategy.

Danielle - Bountiful Bites (Upcycled Snacks)

Danielle viewed marketing through the lens of mission and education. Because her upcycled snack brand centered around sustainability, much of her early marketing focused on explaining the larger problem her company was trying to solve. Danielle became skilled at values-based communication, community engagement, and mission-driven partnerships. Her challenge was learning how to balance purpose with product. Over time, she recognized that consumers needed to understand not only why the mission mattered, but also why the product itself tasted good, fit their lifestyle, and deserved repeat purchase.

Andre - Kindred Grains
(Ancient Grain Snacks)

Andre approached marketing conservatively at first. His natural instinct was to focus on product quality and operational execution, assuming those elements would speak for themselves. As he entered more competitive retail environments, he realized that even excellent products need active communication and visibility. Andre gradually became more comfortable with marketing concepts such as positioning, shopper behavior, and consumer relevance. Rather than chasing trends, he focused on clear messaging, educational content, and disciplined promotional activity that aligned with the brand's long-term identity.

CHAPTER THREE

Trade Marketing

Most founders think about marketing in terms of reaching the consumer, but before you can win over shoppers, you have to win over the trade: retailers, distributors, and industry decision-makers. That's where trade marketing comes in.

Trade marketing refers to promotional activities directed at the trade (distributors, retailers, brokers, foodservice buyers) rather than end consumers. The goal is to build awareness, credibility, and preference within the industry so that your product gains the distribution it needs to reach shelves. Without it, even the best consumer campaigns may fall flat if the trade doesn't know, trust, or support your brand.

Trade marketing builds the foundation for distribution by:

- Getting in front of key decision-makers.

- Demonstrating professionalism and industry presence.

- Showing that you're invested in supporting retailers and distributors.

- Differentiating your brand from the hundreds of others fighting for attention.

Trade Associations: Access, Credibility, and Industry Connection

Trade associations are member-based organizations that represent industries, categories, or special interest groups within the food sector. They function as hubs for education, advocacy, networking, and visibility, bringing together brands, retailers, distributors, service providers, and policymakers. For founders, the right trade association can act as a shortcut to industry knowledge and relationships that would otherwise take years to build independently.

These organizations are especially valuable because they connect founders to the people and information that shape the industry. Through events, committees, and member directories, associations create natural networking opportunities with buyers, distributors, brokers, and fellow founders. They also offer education in the form of workshops, webinars, and research reports tailored to food entrepreneurs navigating regulatory, operational, and commercial challenges. Many associations amplify member brands through newsletters, awards, curated showcases, and speaking opportunities, while also advocating on behalf of members in policy or regulatory discussions.

. . .

One of the most important, and often overlooked, realities of trade associations is that they frequently serve as gatekeepers to some of the industry's most valuable opportunities. Many major trade shows, sponsorship programs, exhibitor opportunities, advertising platforms, and member showcases are either exclusive to members or priced significantly higher for non-members. In some cases, non-members may not be permitted to participate at all.

For example, associations often organize the industry's flagship trade events and reserve priority booth selection, discounted exhibitor pricing, sponsorship access, advertising opportunities, and member directories for companies within their network. Membership can also unlock access to private networking receptions, buyer matchmaking programs, educational sessions, and media visibility opportunities that are not available to the general public.

This matters because trade shows and association-led events are not simply networking opportunities, they are often where critical industry relationships begin. Buyers, distributors, brokers, investors, and media frequently rely on these association ecosystems to identify emerging brands and trends. Brands operating outside of these networks may find themselves at a disadvantage when trying to gain visibility or credibility.

Practical benefits often include discounted trade show rates, co-op marketing opportunities, member advertising rates, and access to group services such as insurance, logistics support, or category data. Over time, the savings and opportunities associated with membership can easily outweigh the annual dues.

There is a wide range of food industry trade associations, each serving different needs. The Specialty Food Association supports gourmet and specialty brands and organizes the Fancy Food Show. The Plant Based Foods Association focuses on advocacy and visibility for plant-based products, while the Organic Trade Association serves certified organic companies with resources and lobbying efforts. Broader organizations like the Consumer Brands Association represent packaged food and beverage companies at scale, while the National Association of Convenience Stores is particularly relevant for snack and beverage brands targeting convenience channels. Many founders also benefit from category-specific groups tied to beverages, confectionery, frozen foods, sustainability, regional agriculture, or minority-owned businesses.

To get real value from trade associations, founders should be selective and intentional. Joining one or two organizations that closely align with your category or growth stage is usually more effective than spreading yourself thin across many. Membership dues can range from a few hundred dollars to five figures annually, so it's important to budget realistically and view the expense as a strategic investment rather than a passive subscription.

Engagement is what transforms membership into opportunity. Attending events, volunteering for committees, participating in webinars, sponsoring programs, or contributing to member communications helps founders build visibility within the industry. Many associations also host their own expos, summits, award programs, and buyer showcases, which can become meaningful extensions of a broader trade show and marketing strategy.

Founders who actively participate tend to stand out more quickly. Committee involvement creates visibility with seasoned industry professionals, while speaking opportunities position founders as thoughtful voices rather than simply product sellers. Awards such as "Best New Product" or "Rising Star" can strengthen credibility with buyers and media. Cross-membership with associations focused on sustainability, diversity, or innovation can also reinforce a broader brand narrative.

In the short term, trade associations provide access to information, discounts, exposure, and industry resources. Over time, they help facilitate deeper relationships with distributors, brokers, retailers, and peers who can influence growth. Long term, consistent involvement helps establish your company as a credible and engaged participant in the industry, strengthening trust and opening doors that are often difficult to access from the outside.

Key Food CPG Trade Associations

Here are some of the most prominent and influential trade associations for food CPG companies in the United States, organized by relevance and specialization. These organizations are especially important because many of them control or heavily influence access to major trade shows, sponsorship opportunities, education programs, networking ecosystems, awards, and industry visibility.

Broad Food & CPG Industry Associations

Specialty Food Association
One of the most valuable organizations for emerging and premium food brands. Organizer of the Fancy Food Show and well known for networking, buyer access, education, trend forecasting, and the Sofi Awards.

Consumer Brands Association
Formerly the Grocery Manufacturers Association (GMA), this is one of the largest trade organizations representing packaged food, beverage, household, and consumer goods companies. Strong focus on advocacy, policy, regulation, and large-scale CPG industry issues.

FMI – The Food Industry Association
One of the most important organizations for grocery retail and food distribution. FMI connects retailers, wholesalers, suppliers, and service providers and is highly influential in food retail operations, shopper insights, food safety, and supply chain discussions.

Natural, Organic, and Better-for-You Associations

Organic Trade Association

Focused on certified organic companies, advocacy, regulation, and industry standards for the organic sector. Particularly important for brands built around organic positioning.

Plant Based Foods Association

One of the leading organizations supporting plant-based food companies through advocacy, education, consumer research, and retailer visibility.

Natural Products Association

A major organization representing natural products, supplements, health foods, and wellness-oriented brands. Particularly relevant for functional food and natural channel companies.

Retail & Channel-Specific Associations

National Association of Convenience Stores

Commonly known as NACS, this is one of the most influential organizations for brands targeting convenience retail and grab-and-go channels. Organizer of the major NACS Show.

National Restaurant Association

Primarily restaurant-focused, but highly relevant for foodservice brands, ingredient suppliers, and manufacturers targeting QSR and hospitality channels.

International Fresh Produce Association

One of the largest organizations supporting the produce and fresh supply chain sectors globally. Particularly important for refrigerated, produce-adjacent, and fresh food companies.

Category-Specific Associations

Depending on the product category, founders may also benefit from joining specialized organizations such as:

- International Dairy Foods Association
- National Coffee Association
- American Frozen Food Institute
- American Spice Trade Association
- Institute of Food Technologists
- Association of Food Industries
- International Bottled Water Association

These groups often provide highly targeted education, networking, regulatory support, and category-specific trade events.

Organization	Primary Focus	Best For	Key Benefits	Major Events / Platforms
Specialty Food Association	Specialty and premium food products	Emerging and established specialty food brands	Buyer access, trend insights, awards, networking, education	Fancy Food Show, Sofi Awards
Consumer Brands Association	Broad packaged goods and consumer products	Large-scale CPG brands and growth-stage companies	Advocacy, policy influence, regulatory resources, industry networking	Industry leadership forums and policy events
FMI – The Food Industry Association	Grocery retail and food distribution	Brands targeting grocery retail and supply chain growth	Retailer access, shopper insights, food safety education, supply chain resources	FMI Midwinter Executive Conference
Organic Trade Association	Organic food and agriculture	Certified organic brands	Organic advocacy, regulatory guidance, networking, market data	Organic industry events and summits
Plant Based Foods Association	Plant-based foods and beverages	Plant-based and alternative protein brands	Retail advocacy, category insights, media exposure, networking	Plant-based industry showcases

Table: Key Trade Associations

Organization	Primary Focus	Best For	Key Benefits	Major Events / Platforms
National Association of Convenience Stores	Convenience retail and grab-and-go channels	Snack, beverage, and impulse-item brands	C-store buyer access, merchandising education, networking	NACS Show
National Restaurant Association	Foodservice and hospitality	Foodservice-foc used brands and ingredient suppliers	Restaurant operator access, foodservice education, industry advocacy	National Restaurant Association Show
Institute of Food Technologists	Food science and innovation	R&D-driven brands and technical founders	Product development education, technical resources, innovation networking	IFT FIRST Annual Event
International Fresh Produce Association	Fresh produce and perishables	Fresh, refrigerated, and produce-adjacen t brands	Produce supply chain access, sustainability resources, buyer networking	Global Produce & Floral Show
American Frozen Food Institute	Frozen food industry	Frozen meal, snack, and dessert brands	Frozen category advocacy, logistics education, regulatory support	AFFI Frozen Food Convention

Table: Key Trade Association Cont'd

Why These Organizations Matter

For founders, trade associations are far more than networking groups. They often function as industry ecosystems that provide:

- Access to buyers and distributors
- Priority t rade show participation and discounted booth rates
- Sponsorship and advertising opportunities
- Educational programming and market research
- Awards and visibility programs
- Regulatory and advocacy support
- Industry credibility and relationship building

Many associations prioritize members for exhibitor space, sponsorships, speaking opportunities, and media visibility. In some cases, non-members either cannot participate or must pay significantly higher rates. This makes association membership a vital and strategic access point into the industry itself.

154

Pro Tip: Treat association membership as a strategic investment, not simply a line item. Many of the food industry's most valuable trade shows, sponsorship opportunities, advertising platforms, and networking events are built around association ecosystems. Founders who actively participate gain far more than discounts, they gain access, visibility, and credibility within the industry.

Trade Shows

Trade shows sit at the intersection of visibility and strategy within trade marketing. They are not designed for direct consumer selling, but for connecting brands with the buyers, distributors, and partners who control access to shelf space. Trade shows are industry gatherings designed for brands to build relationships with the gatekeepers of retail: buyers, distributors, brokers, category managers, and industry media. When used strategically, they can accelerate distribution, validate positioning, and signal credibility. When used prematurely, they can drain cash with little return.

Retailers attend trade shows to scout innovation, fill category gaps, and assess whether a brand is truly retail-ready. Distributors and brokers use them to identify brands worth representing. Simply showing up, especially at the right show for your category and stage, communicates seriousness and intent in a way that cold outreach rarely does.

Trade shows should be viewed as long-term relationship builders, not quick wins. Many meaningful retail relationships begin with a brief booth conversation, followed by months of follow-up, data sharing, and operational readiness before a test ever launches.

Major Trade Shows Food
Founders Should Understand

Not every show is right for every brand. Category fit, budget, and stage of growth matter. Below are some of the most relevant trade shows and buyer forums across food retail channels:

Natural Products Expo West
The largest natural and organic trade show in the U.S. Essential for better-for-you, wellness, and emerging brands seeking visibility with national and regional buyers.

Summer Fancy Food Show
Hosted by the Specialty Food Association, focused on gourmet, premium, and specialty food brands with strong attendance from specialty, independent, and upscale retail buyers.

Winter FancyFaire
Formerly the Winter Fancy Food Show, now a more curated, experience-driven event that often allows for deeper, more intentional buyer conversations.

PLMA (Private Label Manufacturers Association)
A critical event for brands exploring private label, co-manufacturing, or retailer-owned brand opportunities.

Sweets & Snacks Expo
Category-specific to confectionery and snacks, with strong emphasis on innovation, packaging, and emerging trends.

IDDBA (International Dairy Deli Bakery Association) Show
Essential for brands in dairy, cheese, bakery, deli, and perimeter-store categories.

ECRM Sessions
Not a traditional trade show, but curated, category-specific buyer meetings. Highly effective for targeted pitches and early retail access without the cost of large booths.

The NACS Show
The leading trade event for the convenience channel, ideal for brands focused on on-the-go formats, beverages, snacks, and food-service-adjacent retail.

Distributor Shows (UNFI, KeHE, and others)
Often invite-only, regional events that are critical for brands already working with, or pitching, distributors. These shows can directly impact whether your product is prioritized in a distributor's catalog.

Regional and Niche Shows
Including Good Food Mercantile, Plant Based World, Expo Comida Latina, KosherFest, and other culturally or category-specific events. These can offer strong ROI when tightly aligned with your product and consumer.

Planning for Trade Shows as a Trade Investment

Trade shows are a form of trade spend and should be budgeted accordingly. Booth fees, travel, samples, staffing, and collateral add up quickly. Major shows like Expo West can easily require a $20,000–$40,000 all-in investment, even for a modest presence.

Founders should plan several months ahead, not just financially but strategically. That includes identifying which buyers attend which shows, setting meetings in advance, preparing sell sheets and pricing, and aligning production so samples accurately reflect what will ship at scale.

If a booth is not financially realistic, walking the show can still be a powerful learning and networking experience. Many early-stage founders gain more insight from observing buyer behavior, competitor positioning, and category trends than they would from standing behind a booth too early.

Trade Shows and ROI Expectations

The return on trade shows is rarely immediate. Short-term outcomes include leads, follow-up meetings, broker introductions, and distributor conversations. Medium-term results may show up as test placements or regional authorization months later. Long-term value comes from repeated presence and recognition. Buyers often need to see a brand multiple times before trusting it with shelf space.

Trade shows reward preparedness, not presence. The brands that win aren't always the loudest or flashiest. Sometimes they're the ones that show up with clear pricing, realistic distribution plans, operational readiness, and the patience to build relationships over time.

Pro Tip: If you can't afford a booth, don't sit out. Walk the floor with samples, network strategically, and soak up market knowledge. For early-stage founders, that learning can be more valuable than any single order.

BONUS - How to Budget for a Trade Show

For many founders, their first trade show is both exciting and over-whelming. It's the moment your brand steps out from behind the spreadsheets, recipes, and small retail wins to present itself on a much bigger stage.

To bring this to life, let's imagine a hypothetical event: The Flavor First Show in San Diego, CA. This is the very first trade show that two very different startups are preparing to exhibit at. Both are eager to make a strong impression, but their resources look very different.

- One is a bootstrap brand, operating on a tight budget, that secured a modest 10x10 booth. With limited cash, they opted for the essentials: a pop-up banner, the basic table and chairs provided in the booth package, and carefully portioned samples.

- The other is a well-funded startup backed by investors that invested in a 20x20 custom-built booth. Their strategy includes hiring brand ambassadors, designing a premium booth experience, and ordering thousands of branded tote bags to give away to visitors.

Both companies face real costs that go beyond the booth fee: shipping, travel, union labor, furnishings, and the samples themselves. And both have to navigate the learning curve of their big debut.

What follows are two realistic trade show budgets, one lean and scrappy, the other fully loaded, to illustrate how different financial approaches shape the same milestone moment.

Assumptions for *Flavor First Show* in San Diego, CA

- **Booth fee:** $39 per sq. ft. (first-time exhibitor rate).

- **Minimal budget scenario:** 10x10 booth (100 sq. ft.) → $3,900 booth fee.

- **Well-funded scenario:** 20x20 booth (400 sq. ft.) → $15,600 booth fee.

MINIMAL BUDGET

Trade shows can be one of the most effective ways to introduce your brand to buyers, brokers, and industry partners, but they require thoughtful financial planning. Even a modest presence involves multiple cost layers beyond the booth fee itself, including logistics, staffing, sampling, and basic marketing materials.

The example below outlines a lean, entry-level approach to exhibiting at a major show. It reflects the minimum investment required to present your brand professionally while managing costs carefully. For many early-stage founders, this level of participation is enough to gain exposure, begin building relationships, and test how the market responds before committing to larger, more elaborate activations in future shows.

Minimal Budget

10x10 Booth, Pop-Up Banner, Basic Table/Furnishings

Expense Category	Estimated Cost	Notes
Booth Fee	**$3,900**	100 sq. ft. × $39
Furnishings (basic package)	**$500**	Table, 2 chairs, wastebasket (often bundled)
Pop-Up Banner	**$300**	Simple retractable banner with logo/brand story
Carpet (required)	**$400**	Some shows mandate floor covering
Samples (product + prep)	**$1,500**	1,500 sample units for booth visitors
Shipping product/materials	**$600**	Ground freight to San Diego + drayage (union move-in/out)
Marketing Collateral	**$400**	Sell sheets, price lists, business cards
Travel (2 staff, 3 nights)	**$2,400**	Flights $400 × 2, Hotel $250 × 3 nights × 2 rooms
Meals and Incidentals	**$600**	Per diem for 2 staff
Misc. Show Services	**$300**	Electrical outlet, wi-fi (if not included)
TOTAL	**$10,900**	Lean, but professional presence

Table: Minimal Trade Show Budget Scenario

WELL-FUNDED BUDGET

For brands with greater resources, trade shows can become more than a point of presence, they become a stage for storytelling, visibility, and momentum. A larger footprint, custom booth design, and expanded staffing allow companies to create an immersive brand experience that attracts attention and drives engagement at scale.

The example below reflects a fully built-out activation designed to maximize impact. Investments extend beyond space into design, labor, giveaways, and technology, all working together to increase traffic, capture leads, and reinforce brand positioning. While the financial commitment is significantly higher, this level of execution can accelerate brand recognition, strengthen buyer relationships, and generate meaningful post-show opportunities when paired with a clear strategy and follow-through.

Well-Funded Budget

20x20 Booth, Custom Exhibit, Brand Ambassadors, Premium Giveaways

Expense Category	Estimated Cost	Notes
Booth Fee	**$15,600**	400 sq. ft. × $39
Custom Booth Design and Fabrication	**$40,000**	Custom build + graphics, often reused for multiple shows
Booth Labor (Union Install/Dismantle)	**$8,000**	Larger booths require union labor; billed hourly
Furnishings and Carpet	**$3,000**	Premium seating, tables, storage, upgraded flooring
Brand Ambassadors (4 × 3 days)	**$6,000**	$500/day + agency fees
Tote Bag Giveaways (2,500 units)	**$7,500**	$3.00 each with logo
Samples (product + prep)	**$5,000**	6,000 units for giveaways and in-booth tastings
Shipping product/materials	**$3,500**	Freight + drayage for larger setup
AV/Technology	**$2,500**	Screens, looping video, iPads for lead capture

Table: Well-Funded Trade Show Budget Scenario

Marketing Collateral	$1,500	Premium brochures, catalogs, QR-coded digital kits
Travel (6 staff, 4 nights)	$12,000	Flights $500 × 6, Hotel $300 × 4 nights × 6 rooms
Meals and Incidentals	$4,000	Staff + ambassador per diems
Misc. Show Services	$2,500	Electrical, wi-fi, waste handling
TOTAL	**$111,100**	Fully-loaded, high-visibility presence

Table: Well-Funded Trade Show Budget Scenario Continued

TRADE SHOW PLANNING TIMELINE

Strong execution at trade shows is rarely accidental. The brands that generate meaningful results are typically following a structured timeline that aligns production, logistics, marketing, and outreach well in advance. Because so many moving parts are involved, from booth design and sampling to travel and buyer meetings, timing becomes just as important as budget.

A well-planned timeline allows founders to secure better rates, avoid last-minute rush fees, and ensure that every detail, from product availability to staffing, is executed with intention. It also creates space for proactive outreach, which is often the difference between simply showing up and walking away with real opportunities. Buyers' schedules fill quickly, and brands that plan early are far more likely to secure time on calendars rather than relying on chance foot traffic.

The timeline that follows outlines a practical cadence for preparing for a major industry show. While exact timing may vary depending on the event and the complexity of your activation, this framework helps ensure that nothing critical is overlooked and that your investment translates into a well-executed, high-impact presence.

BONUS - Trade Show Planning Timeline

6–12 Months Before

- Research shows, apply for booth space, pay deposit.
- Decide booth size and design (start fabrication if custom).
- Apply for new product showcases or award competitions.

4–6 Months Before

- Book travel and hotel (rates climb quickly).
- Plan sampling strategy (decide SKUs, serving method, portioning).
- Order collateral (sell sheets, banners, signage).
- Coordinate with co-packer for production runs timed to the show.

2–3 Months Before

- Finalize shipping logistics for booth materials and samples.
- Submit exhibitor service orders (electricity, internet, labor, carpet).
- Reach out to buyers to schedule meetings during the show.
- Hire brand ambassadors if using them.
- Order giveaways (ex., tote bags).

1 Month Before

- Train your staff: practice 30-second pitch, FAQ handling.
- Test booth set up (if custom).
- Print/collate collateral.
- Ship dry goods and displays to show warehouse.

Figure: BONUS - Trade Show Planning Timeline

1–2 Weeks Before

- Confirm freight delivery and drayage schedule.

- Pack sample shipments (cold chain for perishables if needed).

- Send calendar invites to buyers you've scheduled.

- Post on LinkedIn/social to announce your presence at Flavor First.

During the Show

- Arrive early to set up and troubleshoot.

- Track leads and scan badges digitally.

- Restock booth daily and monitor sampling levels.

- Walk the floor for competitor intel and networking.

After the Show (1–2 Weeks)

- Follow up with all leads within 3-5 business days via email and/or LinkedIn.

- Send physical thank-you notes to buyers you met.

- Debrief internally: what worked, what didn't, ROI vs. spend.

- Decide if you'll rebook for next year.

Figure: BONUS - Trade Show Planning Timeline Continued

IMPORTANT NOTE ON EXHIBIT DISPLAYS

Exhibit displays are not a "single use" expense, they're an investment. Whether it's a simple pop-up banner or a custom 20x20 booth, most brands use their displays at multiple shows and events over several years.

. . .

Minimal Budget Scenario:

- The $300 pop-up banner and basic booth furnishings are modest but portable.

- Expect to use these at 3–5 shows (trade, distributor shows, local events) before refreshing.

- Amortized cost: $60–100 per show instead of $300 upfront.

Well-Funded Scenario:

- The $40,000 custom booth is built for durability and modularity. Panels and components can be reconfigured for different booth sizes (10x20, 20x20, 20x30).

- Most brands use custom booths for 3–5 years, across 5–10 shows annually.

- Amortized cost: roughly $1,000–2,500 per show, depending on frequency, not $40K per event.

Pro Tip: When presenting budgets to investors or board members, make sure to highlight that custom exhibit costs are amortized over multiple events. This frames them as capital investments in brand visibility, not one-time marketing splurges.

Trade Publications

Trade publications are industry-specific magazines, websites, and newsletters read by buyers, distributors, brokers, category managers, and other food industry professionals. Advertising in these outlets is not designed to influence the end consumer. Instead, it speaks directly to the gatekeepers who decide which products are reviewed, ranged, promoted, and ultimately placed on shelves. For early-stage and growing CPG brands, trade advertising is about visibility within the industry itself, not consumer demand generation.

The primary value of advertising in trade publications is targeted exposure to decision-makers. Buyers often scan these publications to stay current on category trends, emerging brands, and innovation, even if only briefly. A well-timed ad, feature, or product mention helps keep your brand top of mind during category reviews or buyer meetings. Appearing consistently in respected trade outlets also builds credibility. It signals that your brand is serious, prepared for retail, and participating in the broader industry conversation rather than operating in isolation.

Beyond traditional display ads, many trade publications offer opportunities for deeper storytelling through editorial features, Q&As, sponsored content, or "new product" sections. These formats can be especially valuable for founders because they allow you to explain not just what the product is, but why it exists, how it fits into a category, and what problem it solves. In many cases, these options are more cost-effective than large print ads and can feel more authentic and informative to industry readers.

Planning for trade publication advertising requires intentionality. Founders should first identify which publications align with their category and channel focus, whether that's grocery, natural, specialty, beverage, or convenience. Budgets can vary widely, from a few thousand dollars for digital placements to five figures for premium print exposure, so timing and scale matter. Coordinating placements around major industry moments, such as trade shows or seasonal category resets, can significantly improve impact. It's also worth exploring alternatives to paid ads, including press releases, contributed articles, or product announcements, which can deliver visibility with lower financial commitment.

Standing out in a trade publication environment requires clarity and restraint. Strong visuals that clearly show the product, paired with a concise headline, tend to perform better than dense copy. Buyers want to understand what the product is, who it's for, and why it matters within seconds. A clear call to action, whether directing readers to a website, trade show booth, or distributor, helps convert awareness into next steps. Consistency is equally important. One-off ads are rarely effective, but repeated exposure over time builds recognition and familiarity.

The outcomes of trade publication advertising tend to unfold in stages. In the short term, brands may see increased inbound interest from buyers, brokers, or distributors requesting samples or meetings. Over the medium term, consistent presence can support inclusion in category reviews or assortment discussions. Long term, trade advertising helps establish your brand as a recognizable player within its category, strengthening your overall sales narrative when paired with performance data and retail execution.

Examples of Food Industry Trade Publications:

- **Progressive Grocer** – Widely read by grocery executives and decision-makers.

- **Supermarket News** – Covers trends, retail innovation, and new product launches.

- **Winsight Grocery Business** – Insights for grocery and C-store professionals.

- **BevNET** – Beverage-specific coverage, including product launches and funding news.

- **NOSH** – Focuses on natural, organic, sustainable, and healthy CPG brands.

- **Local/Regional Outlets** – State-level agricultural publications or regional distributor newsletters.

Pro Tip: Don't think of trade ads as standalone marketing. Pair them with PR outreach, show attendance, and distributor programs for maximum effect. A buyer is far more likely to remember you if they've seen your ad, walked past your booth, and tasted your product all in the same season.

Trade Event Sponsorships

Sponsoring industry events involves providing financial support, product donations, or in-kind contributions to trade shows, conferences, award ceremonies, or networking gatherings in exchange for brand visibility and access to key decision-makers. Unlike exhibiting at a trade show, sponsorships often place your brand in front of the industry in more subtle but powerful ways, such as being featured on stage, included in event materials, highlighted in digital promotions, or incorporated into attendee experiences like gift bags or tastings. For many founders, sponsorship is a way to participate in the industry conversation without the full cost and logistics of a booth.

The value of sponsorship lies largely in perception and proximity. When your logo appears alongside established brands, respected organizations, or influential industry voices, it elevates how your company is viewed. Sponsorship signals commitment and credibility, showing that you are investing in the industry rather than simply trying to extract value from it. Many sponsorships also include built-in networking advantages, such as VIP access, private receptions, or curated introductions, creating environments where buyers, investors, and partners are more relaxed and approachable. At higher levels, sponsorships may offer thought leadership opportunities through panels, speaking slots, or hosted sessions that allow you to share your perspective and story directly.

In the food industry, sponsorship opportunities range widely in scope and cost. National award galas hosted by trade associations can position your brand alongside innovation leaders, while conferences focused on food technology, sustainability, or emerging categories allow you to align with broader industry trends. Category-specific awards provide targeted exposure within your niche, while local or regional events often offer high-impact visibility at a much lower investment. Partnerships with universities, culinary schools, or incubators can also reinforce credibility while connecting you to future talent and innovation ecosystems.

Planning a sponsorship should start with a clear understanding of your goals. Some founders are seeking visibility, others credibility, and others access to relationships. The right sponsorship aligns with what you need most at your current stage. Budgets can range from a few hundred dollars for local events to tens of thousands for national conferences, so early-stage brands are often best served by smaller, focused opportunities where their presence feels meaningful rather than diluted. It's also critical to fully leverage what's included, whether that's attendee lists, social media mentions, sampling opportunities, or stage time.

Standing out as a sponsor requires more than just writing a check. Sampling can turn abstract brand awareness into a tangible experience, especially in food. Thoughtful giveaways that feel useful or memorable reinforce recall long after the event ends. If given a microphone, founders should focus on authentic, concise storytelling rather than sales pitches. And when access to attendees or leads is provided, timely follow-up is essential. The true return on sponsorship often depends on what happens after the event, not during it.

The outcomes of event sponsorships tend to compound over time. In the short term, brands gain visibility and recognition among industry insiders, along with potential introductions to buyers or partners. Over the medium term, sponsorships can lead to press mentions, award consideration, or inclusion in category conversations. Long term, consistent participation helps establish your brand as a serious, engaged player in the industry, not just another product seeking shelf space.

Pro Tip: Sponsorships work best when paired with in-person presence at the event. Don't just pay for logo placement, show up, shake hands, and make the most of the exposure you've paid for.

Distributor Visibility Programs

Distributor visibility programs are paid marketing opportunities within a distributor's ecosystem designed to surface your product to retailers who rely on distributor catalogs, flyers, portals, and promotions to discover new items. Because distributors manage thousands, sometimes tens of thousands, of SKUs, these programs help ensure your product doesn't disappear into the warehouse unnoticed. Instead of being just another line item in a catalog, your brand is placed directly in front of buyers when they are actively looking for products to add, refresh, or promote on their shelves.

These programs matter because distributors are often the first filter between your brand and the retailer. Without added visibility, even strong products can struggle to gain traction simply because buyers never notice them. Being featured by a distributor helps your brand break through the noise, accelerates discovery among independent and regional retailers, and lends credibility to your sales pitch. Retailers frequently ask brands how they are supporting the distributor relationship, and participation in visibility programs shows that you are investing in sell-through, not just placement.

Visibility opportunities take many forms. Distributors commonly feature brands in new product catalogs that introduce recently onboarded SKUs, as well as seasonal flyers tied to holidays or key selling periods. Many host regional or national buying shows, which function like mini trade shows where retailers meet brands and place orders directly. Other programs include promotional offers, such as case discounts or free-fill incentives, and digital placements within distributor portals, email newsletters, or ordering platforms.

Costs vary depending on the type and scale of the program, but they should be treated as a planned component of trade spend rather than a surprise expense. Flyer insertions typically run in the hundreds to low thousands per issue, catalog features can reach several thousand dollars, and distributor trade shows range from a few thousand for regional events to well into five figures for national programs. Promotional allowances during these initiatives often require temporary discounts of 10–20 percent off invoice. For most brands, these investments are mapped out annually as part of a broader distributor and retail support strategy.

To maximize impact, visibility programs work best when they are timed thoughtfully. Aligning distributor promotions with category review periods increases the likelihood that buyers will act. Pairing visibility with sampling, whether through free cases or coordinated demos, can help translate awareness into velocity. Tracking performance data from these programs is critical, as strong results can be reused in future pitches and negotiations. It's also worth asking distributors about bundled packages, as combining flyers, shows, and digital placements often delivers better value than purchasing each element separately.

In the short term, distributor visibility programs often lead to increased orders from independent retailers scanning catalogs or attending buying shows. Over time, they can help establish traction in new regions and demonstrate repeat demand at smaller accounts. Long term, consistent participation strengthens your relationship with the distributor and creates leverage when negotiating expanded coverage, better support, or more favorable terms as your brand grows.

• • •

Pro Tip: Distributor visibility programs can feel like "pay to play," but they are a powerful way to jumpstart sales velocity. The key is to plan and budget for them, don't treat them as an afterthought when a distributor rep suggests it mid-year.

Our Founders' Journey

Elena - Harbor Harvest Foods (Spiced Mango Preserves)

Elena approached trade marketing cautiously and strategically. Her spiced mango preserves performed well in specialty retail, but she knew her resources were limited. Rather than pursuing aggressive expansion, Elena focused on strengthening relationships with a small group of independent retailers and regional specialty accounts. She invested selectively in trade shows, retailer presentations, and simple but polished sales materials. By maintaining strong communication and consistent support, she built credibility slowly, proving that a smaller brand could still operate professionally within the trade environment.

Marcus - Summit Sips (Clean Labeled Sparkling Iced Tea)

Marcus viewed trade marketing as a growth accelerator. His clean-labeled sparkling iced tea entered retail with ambitious expansion goals, requiring aggressive support across multiple channels. Marcus allocated significant resources toward slotting fees, distributor incentives, trade advertising, and large-scale trade show participation. He quickly learned that retail placement alone was not enough, buyers expected ongoing investment and measurable support. For Marcus, trade marketing became deeply tied to maintaining retailer confidence and protecting shelf space in a highly competitive beverage category.

Danielle - Bountiful Bites (Upcycled Snacks)

Danielle approached trade marketing through mission alignment and storytelling. Her upcycled snack brand attracted interest from natural and sustainability-focused retailers, but she still needed to prove commercial viability. Danielle focused on association memberships, sustainability conferences, and mission-driven trade events where her brand narrative resonated strongly. She also invested in educational sales materials that helped buyers understand both the product and the larger sustainability movement behind it. Her strategy reinforced that trade marketing is not always about the largest budget, but about finding the right audience and communicating value clearly.

Andre - Kindred Grains
(Ancient Grain Snacks)

Andre took a measured, relationship-first approach. His ancient grain snacks gained traction gradually, and he used trade marketing to reinforce operational credibility rather than create hype. Andre prioritized category reviews, distributor conversations, and retailer meetings supported by clean data, strong forecasting, and realistic growth plans. He avoided overcommitting to expensive programs too early, instead focusing on targeted trade investments that aligned with accounts already showing strong performance. His strategy reflected discipline and long-term thinking.

CHAPTER FOUR

Shopper Marketing

Getting onto the shelf is a milestone. Getting off the shelf is what matters.

Shopper marketing is where strategy and the moment of decision meet. It encompasses all of the in-store and retailer-connected touchpoints that influence a consumer as they browse, compare, and choose what to buy. Unlike brand marketing, which builds awareness over time, shopper marketing is designed to convert, often within seconds.

In the CPG environment, most purchase decisions are made quickly and with limited information. Shoppers are scanning, not studying. They are comparing price, packaging, placement, and promotions in real time. Your product is not being evaluated in isolation, it is being judged against everything around it. This is where shopper marketing becomes essential.

Every element inside the store plays a role. Shelf tags signal value. End caps create visibility. Circulars and apps shape intent before the shopper even walks through the door. Sampling removes hesitation. Coupons and loyalty programs influence price perception. Together, these tools create a system that either supports your product or leaves it to compete on packaging alone.

For founders, shopper marketing is also where investment begins to show up in measurable ways. Retailers are not just looking at whether your product is listed, they are looking at how it performs. Strong shopper marketing drives trial, increases velocity, and supports reorders. Weak execution can result in slow movement, regardless of how strong the product may be.

This chapter focuses on the practical tools that influence shopper behavior in-store and across connected digital channels. The goal is not to do everything at once, but to understand how each element works and how to apply them strategically as your brand grows.

In-Store Demos / Sampling

In-store demos and sampling remain some of the most effective tools in shopper marketing because they remove one of the biggest barriers to purchase: uncertainty. When consumers can taste, smell, or experience a product before buying it, hesitation decreases and confidence increases.

For emerging brands especially, sampling creates an opportunity to introduce the product directly to the shopper in a way that packaging and signage alone cannot. A strong demo allows consumers to experience flavor, texture, aroma, and quality in real time, often turning curiosity into immediate purchase.

Unlike broad awareness marketing, demos are highly targeted. They take place at the exact location where the product can be purchased, which makes them one of the clearest examples of working dollars in action. When executed well, demos can drive measurable lift during and after the activation period.

Why Sampling Works

Food purchasing is deeply sensory. Consumers may understand a product concept intellectually, but tasting the product creates emotional and physical confirmation. This is particularly important for:

- New products
- Premium products
- Functional foods and beverages
- Better-for-you alternatives
- Unique flavors or textures

Sampling helps overcome skepticism and allows shoppers to evaluate the product for themselves.

It also creates a human connection. A knowledgeable, engaging demo representative can answer questions, explain benefits, and reinforce the brand story in a way that static marketing materials cannot.

What Makes a Strong Demo Program

Successful demos require more than simply handing out samples. Execution matters.

Staffing and Representation

The person representing the product should be professional, approachable, and knowledgeable about the brand. They are not just serving samples, they are representing the company in real time.

Product Presentation

The setup should be clean, organized, and visually aligned with the brand. Sampling stations should feel intentional and professional, regardless of scale.

Clear Messaging

Shoppers should quickly understand what the product is, why it is different, and where it is located in the store. Messaging should be concise and easy to communicate in conversation.

. . .

Retail Coordination

Strong demos are coordinated with the store in advance. Inventory should be sufficiently stocked before the activation begins. There is little value in driving interest if the shelf is empty.

Measuring Effectiveness

One of the advantages of in-store demos is that they can often be measured directly. Brands may track:

- Sales lift during the demo period
- Repeat sales in the following weeks
- Sample-to-purchase conversion rates
- Shopper engagement and feedback

This data helps founders understand whether the activation is driving meaningful results and where future investment should be allocated.

Budget Considerations

Sampling programs involve more than just product cost. Founders should plan for:

- Demo staffing or agency fees
- Product sample allocation
- Sampling equipment and supplies
- Transportation and setup costs
- Permits or retailer participation fees (if applicable)

These costs should be evaluated against expected sales lift and broader brand-building value.

. . .

Strategic Use Cases

Demos are particularly effective when tied to:
• New product launches
• Retail expansions
• Promotional periods
• Seasonal programs
• High-traffic weekends or events

They can also support retailer relationships by demonstrating that the brand is actively investing in sell-through and shopper engagement.

Key Takeaway

In-store demos and sampling create one of the most powerful moments in shopper marketing: creating trial at the point of purchase.

For founders, demos are a great opportunity to build trust, gather feedback, and convert awareness into immediate action. When done well, sampling introduces your product and creates believers.

Store Ads and Digital Promotions

Shopper marketing doesn't simply begin and end inside the store. Increasingly, retailers are influencing consumer decisions before shoppers even arrive, through apps, websites, loyalty platforms, email campaigns, and digital advertising ecosystems. For CPG brands, this shift has created new opportunities to reach consumers closer to the point of purchase than ever before.

Store ads and digital promotions allow brands to engage shoppers within a retailer's own environment. These programs can influence search behavior, increase visibility, support promotions, and drive conversion across both physical and digital channels.

Traditional store advertising may include:

- Weekly circulars and flyers
- Featured product placements in retailer emails
- Loyalty card promotions
- In-app coupons and offers

These tools remain highly effective because they reach shoppers who are already planning to purchase groceries. Unlike broader advertising campaigns, retailer-based promotions target consumers who are actively preparing to shop.

The Rise of Retail Media Networks

One of the most significant developments in modern shopper marketing is the growth of Retail Media Networks (RMNs). Retail Media Networks are advertising platforms operated directly by retailers, allowing brands to promote products within the retailer's digital ecosystem.

Major retailers now offer sophisticated advertising platforms that include:

- Sponsored product placements in search results
- Banner ads on retailer websites and apps
- Personalized offers tied to loyalty data
- Off-platform digital advertising using retailer shopper insights

For brands, the power of Retail Media Networks lies in their proximity to purchase. These platforms reach consumers while they are actively shopping or building baskets, making them far more conversion-oriented than traditional awareness advertising.

Retailers also possess valuable first-party shopper data. Because they can see actual purchasing behavior, RMNs allow for highly targeted campaigns based on demographics, purchase history, category behavior, and shopping patterns. This level of targeting makes digital retail advertising increasingly attractive and measurable.

Why Digital Promotions Matter

Digital promotions support both visibility and conversion. They help ensure your product appears in front of shoppers at critical moments, particularly in crowded categories where consumers may otherwise default to familiar brands.

These promotions are especially important for:

- New product launches
- Seasonal campaigns
- Promotional periods
- Retailer-specific initiatives
- Driving awareness in newly expanded markets

They also reinforce physical retail activity. A shopper may first encounter your product through a retailer app or sponsored search result and then purchase it during their next store visit.

Budget and Performance Considerations

While digital retailer programs can be highly effective, they require careful budgeting and performance analysis. Costs may include:

- Sponsored search bidding
- Digital coupon funding
- Featured placement fees
- Retail media campaign management

Like all shopper marketing investments, these programs should be measured against clear objectives. Metrics may include:

- Click-through rates
- Conversion rates
- Basket additions
- Sales lift
- Return on ad spend (ROAS)

Because RMNs operate within the retailer ecosystem, reporting is often stronger and more actionable than traditional digital advertising.

Strategic Considerations for Founders

For emerging brands, digital retailer programs can feel expensive initially, particularly compared to organic marketing channels. However, they are becoming increasingly important as retailers shift more attention and resources toward monetizing their digital platforms.

Founders do not need to participate in every program immediately. The key is understanding where these tools fit within your broader growth strategy. A focused, well-executed campaign tied to a promotion or launch often delivers stronger results than spreading resources too thinly across multiple platforms.

It is also important to coordinate digital promotions with inventory and in-store support. Driving traffic to a product that is out of stock or poorly merchandised undermines both the investment and the consumer experience.

Key Takeaway

Store ads and digital promotions extend shopper marketing beyond the shelf and into the planning and purchasing journey itself.

Retail Media Networks, in particular, are reshaping how brands connect with consumers by combining visibility, targeting, and measurable conversion within the retailer ecosystem. For founders, understanding these platforms is an essential part of competing in modern retail.

Point of Sale (POS) Elements

Getting your product onto the shelf is only the first step. Once it's there, the real challenge begins: capturing a shopper's attention in a crowded aisle and giving them a clear reason to choose your product over familiar competitors. Point of Sale (POS) elements are designed to do exactly that. These tools work at the moment of decision, helping your product stand out, communicate value quickly, and trigger impulse purchases. For many retailers, POS materials are an expected component of promotional support. For founders, they're also one of the most efficient ways to stretch limited marketing dollars by focusing on shoppers when they're already in buying mode.

Shelf Talkers

Shelf talkers are among the most common POS tools you'll encounter. These small signs or tags clip directly onto the shelf edge and call out key attributes such as "New," "Organic," "Gluten-Free," or promotional pricing. They work because they interrupt the visual rhythm of a shelf set, pulling the shopper's eye toward your product. Shelf talkers are especially effective during new SKU launches, when highlighting certifications, or when reinforcing a limited-time promotion that needs to be noticed quickly.

Channel Strips

Channel strips run along the full length of the shelf channel where price tags sit. Instead of calling out a single product, they create a continuous brand presence across multiple facings. Even if your product only has one or two facings, a well-designed channel strip can give the impression of a larger footprint and reinforce brand recognition. These are particularly useful in dense categories where shelves feel cluttered and differentiation is hard to achieve.

Hang Strips

Hang strips place products vertically, often off shelves or end-caps, and typically hold single-serve or trial-size items. By positioning products in high-traffic areas outside the main shelf set, hang strips create additional opportunities for discovery and trial. They're especially effective for snacks, beverages, and other impulse-driven products that benefit from being seen in multiple locations throughout the store.

In-and-Out Displays

In-and-out displays are temporary, freestanding, or pallet-sized displays placed in prominent areas such as store entrances or seasonal aisles. These displays provide valuable secondary placement beyond your primary shelf location and can dramatically increase visibility and volume during promotional periods. They're most often used for seasonal flavors, limited-time offers, or major shopping moments like back-to-school, holidays, or major sporting events.

. . .

POS elements amplify your shelf presence and help level the playing field against larger brands with deeper advertising budgets. Strategic investments in shelf talkers, channel strips, hang strips, and in-and-out displays can significantly boost visibility and trial without relying solely on expensive media campaigns.

As a final note, POS should never exist in a vacuum. The most effective programs align POS elements with your broader promotional calendar, reinforcing demos, temporary price reductions, coupons, or seasonal pushes. When POS supports what's already happening in-store, it becomes a powerful driver of conversion rather than just another sign on the shelf.

Shelf Talkers

Small signs or tags that clip onto the shelf edge, calling out key product attributes (ex., *"New!"*, *"Organic"*, *"Gluten-Free"*) or promotional pricing.

- **Why They Work:** They break up the monotony of a shelf set and draw the eye to your product.
- **Best Use:** Launching new SKUs, highlighting certifications, or tying into a limited-time promotion.

Channel Strips

Printed strips that run along the entire length of a shelf channel (the slot that holds the price tags).

- **Why They Work:** They create a continuous brand impression across multiple facings, even if your product only has one or two spots.
- **Best Use:** Reinforcing branding (logo, color scheme, tagline) in crowded aisles.

Hang Strips

Vertical strips that hang off shelves or end-caps, holding single-serve or trial-size products.

- **Why They Work:** They place your product in high-traffic secondary locations, increasing trial opportunities.
- **Best Use:** Snacks, beverages, or impulse items that benefit from multiple points of availability throughout the store.

In and Out Displays

Temporary freestanding or pallet-sized displays placed in prominent locations (ex., store entrances, seasonal aisles).

- **Why They Work:** They provide secondary placement outside your main shelf set, boosting visibility and sales.
- **Best Use:** Limited-time promotions, seasonal flavors, or campaigns tied to big shopping periods (ex., Super Bowl, Back-to-School, Holidays).

Figure: Point of Sale (POS) Elements

Key Takeaway

POS elements amplify your shelf presence and help level the playing field against larger brands with big advertising budgets. By investing strategically in shelf talkers, channel strips, hang strips, and in-and-out displays, founders can dramatically increase visibility and trial without relying solely on expensive media campaigns.

Pro Tip: Always align POS elements with your promotional calendar. POS should reinforce promotions already happening (TPRs, demos, coupons), not operate in isolation.

BONUS - In and Out Displays

While in-and-out displays can deliver a significant sales lift, they come with retailer-specific rules that founders need to understand. Two of the most common policies that impact how and where displays can be placed are Clean Floor Policy and One Tile Footprint.

Clean Floor Policy

What It Is:
A policy many retailers adopt to keep store aisles free from clutter, ensuring safety and a clean shopping environment. It limits or restricts the placement of free-standing displays outside designated areas.

- Spontaneous placement of displays in aisles is often prohibited.

- Displays are limited to approved zones, such as end-caps, seasonal aisles, or promotional pods.

- Retailers may charge additional fees for placement in premium areas (ex., front-of-store, near checkout).

Always check with your buyer or retailer's merchandising team before creating displays. Designing a display that doesn't comply with a Clean Floor Policy can waste money and risk compliance penalties.

One Tile Footprint

What It Is:

A guideline that restricts the size of temporary displays to the equivalent of one floor tile in the store (often 2x2 feet).

- Prevents displays from sprawling into aisles and blocking traffic.

- Limits the volume of product that can be showcased in each display.

- Encourages brands to design compact, impactful displays that maximize branding in a small footprint.

If you're designing an in-and-out display, work with a display vendor who understands footprint restrictions. A well-designed one-tile display can still stand out with bold graphics, color, and messaging.

Key Takeaway

Both Clean Floor Policies and One Tile Footprints exist to keep stores organized, safe, and shoppable. For founders, they mean you must be strategic and creative in designing displays that comply while still grabbing shopper attention.

Pro Tip: When negotiating display placement, ask:

- *"What's your policy on free-standing displays?"*

- *"Are there size or footprint restrictions I should be aware of?"*

- *"What premium locations are available for in and out displays?"*

By knowing the rules upfront, you can design displays that work *with* the retailer, not against them.

Floor Displays and Shelf-Ready Shippers

While shelf placement is your foundation, floor displays and shelf-ready shippers extend your presence into high-traffic areas of the store. These placements take your product out of the competitive shelf set and position it where shoppers are more likely to notice, engage, and purchase without comparison.

For emerging brands, this is one of the most effective ways to increase visibility and drive incremental sales. When executed well, these displays can introduce your product to new shoppers, support promotions, and reinforce your brand beyond its primary location.

Permanent Displays: Wood and Wire Fixtures

Permanent floor displays are typically constructed from wood or metal wire and are designed for long-term use within the store. These fixtures are often placed in strategic locations such as end caps, aisle intersections, or designated merchandising areas.

Retailers use permanent displays to create consistency and durability in high-traffic environments. For brands, these fixtures offer a more polished and premium presentation. They can elevate perception, particularly for higher-end or specialty products, and may be reused across multiple promotional cycles.

However, permanent displays often require greater investment and coordination. Placement is typically controlled by the retailer, and space may be reserved for established brands or category leaders. When available, these displays can serve as a strong platform for sustained visibility, but they must be supported with consistent inventory and strong sales performance.

Corrugated Displays and Shelf-Ready Shippers

Corrugated displays and shelf-ready shippers are more flexible and widely accessible options, especially for emerging brands. Made from printed cardboard, these displays are designed for short-term use and are often tied to promotions, seasonal programs, or new product launches.

Shelf-ready shippers are particularly valuable because they serve multiple purposes. They are designed to ship product efficiently and then transition directly to the sales floor with minimal handling. This reduces labor for the retailer and increases the likelihood that your product is placed correctly and quickly.

Corrugated displays can be positioned in a variety of locations, including end caps, promotional zones, and secondary placements throughout the store. Their printed surfaces provide an opportunity to communicate brand messaging, highlight key benefits, and reinforce promotional activity.

Because they are temporary, these displays create a sense of urgency. Shoppers recognize that the product is being featured for a limited time, which can encourage trial and impulse purchases.

Strategic Considerations

Floor displays and shelf-ready shippers are most effective when aligned with a clear objective. Whether supporting a promotion, launching a new SKU, or increasing visibility in a key account, these displays should be tied to a specific goal.

Inventory planning is critical. Displays must be well-stocked and maintained to deliver results. An empty or disorganized display can quickly undermine the opportunity and reflect poorly on the brand.

Placement also matters. High-traffic locations drive the greatest impact, but they often require coordination with the retailer and may involve additional trade investment. Understanding how your display fits within the store's merchandising strategy increases the likelihood of success.

Key Takeaway

Floor displays and shelf-ready shippers take your product beyond the shelf and into the flow of the store. They create visibility, support promotions, and introduce your brand to shoppers who may not have been actively searching for it.

Store Promotional Programs

Retailers don't simply place products on shelves and wait for them to sell, they actively drive demand through structured promotional programs. For founders, participation in these programs is rarely optional. Promotions are one of the primary ways to generate trial, increase velocity, and demonstrate to buyers that your brand is worth keeping and expanding. They also signal that you understand how retail works and are willing to invest alongside the retailer to grow the category.

Store promotional programs vary by retailer, but most fall into a handful of familiar formats.

Circulars and Flyers

Circulars and flyers, whether printed or digital, are weekly ads that spotlight discounted products and are especially effective in high-low retail environments where shoppers expect deals. Brands typically pay for placement in these ads, with costs tied to circulation size and ad prominence, but the payoff can be meaningful in terms of traffic and awareness.

Loyalty Program

Loyalty program discounts are another common tool, offering special pricing to shoppers enrolled in a retailer's rewards program. Chains like Kroger and Safeway rely heavily on these programs to personalize offers and drive repeat visits. Brands usually fund part of the discount, but in return gain access to a highly engaged shopper base and, in some cases, post-promotion data insights.

End-cap and Display Promotions

End-cap and display promotions provide secondary placement outside your primary shelf set, often tied to seasonal moments or major events. These placements are highly visible and can dramatically lift sales, but they are also among the most expensive options, frequently requiring display fees, free cases, or additional promotional funding. When executed well, they can introduce your product to shoppers who might never have walked down your aisle.

In-store Signage and Point of Sale (POS) Features

In-store signage and POS features, such as shelf talkers, channel strips, or digital shelf tags, are often bundled with promotions to amplify visibility at the point of decision. These elements help your product stand out in crowded aisles and reinforce the promotional message. Digital promotions, including app-based coupons, banner ads, and push notifications, are becoming increasingly important as omnichannel shopping grows. They extend your reach beyond the physical shelf and influence shoppers before they even enter the store.

These store programs matter because promotions are one of the fastest ways to boost velocity. Temporary price reductions lower the barrier to trial and can quickly demonstrate demand. Participation also strengthens your relationship with the retailer, showing that you're invested in supporting their business rather than simply occupying shelf space. In competitive categories, promotions are often table stakes. If your competitors are actively promoting and you are not, your product risks being overlooked or underperforming by comparison. Promotion calendars also play a role in forecasting and category planning, as retailers often expect brands to commit months in advance, and your participation can influence future resets and shelf allocations.

For founders, the key is to approach store promotional programs strategically. Promotions should be built into your annual trade spend plan from the start, not treated as surprise expenses. Rather than promoting everywhere at once, focus on priority accounts and time promotions around peak seasons or moments that align naturally with your product. Measuring results is essential. Comparing baseline velocity to promotional performance, and tracking whether sales sustain after the discount ends, helps you understand what's working. Whenever possible, pairing promotions with secondary placement multiplies their impact. Used thoughtfully, store promotional programs become a powerful lever for building trial, credibility, and long-term retail success.

Types of Store Promotional Programs

Circulars and Flyers

- Weekly ads (print or digital) that highlight products on promotion.
- Brands typically pay for placement, with costs depending on prominence and distribution size.
- Effective for driving traffic and awareness, especially in High-Low retailers.

Loyalty Card Discounts

- Special pricing offered only to shoppers enrolled in the retailer's loyalty program.
- Retailers like Kroger or Safeway rely heavily on these to personalize offers.
- Brands often fund part of the discount.

End-Cap and Display Promotions

- Secondary placement outside your category, often tied to seasonal or event-based themes.
- Highly visible but expensive, as retailers may charge slotting or display fees.

In-Store Signage and POS Features

- Shelf talkers, channel strips, or digital shelf tags calling out promotions.
- Often bundled with promotional programs to amplify awareness.

Digital Promotions

- Offers featured on the retailer's website or app.
- Examples: digital coupons, banner ads, or retailer push notifications.
- Increasingly important as omnichannel shopping grows.

Figure: Types of Store Promotional Programs

Real-World Simulation

A sparkling water startup participated in a 2-for-$6 store loyalty promotion at a regional grocery chain. During the two-week promo, sales increased by 250%. More importantly, velocities remained 30% higher for the following month, proving the promotion drove trial and repeat purchase.

203

Pro Tip: Always align store promotional programs with your own marketing calendar. A coupon in a retailer's circular is way more effective if it's reinforced by your social media, email campaigns, and in-store demos.

Even the strongest product and most thoughtful packaging won't sell if it isn't properly stocked, faced, and presented on the shelf. That responsibility can be managed by merchandisers, the often unseen but essential players who ensure your product shows up in the right place, in the right quantity, and in the best possible condition. Merchandisers are the link between all the planning that happens on paper and what shoppers actually experience in-store, making them a critical part of retail execution.

Merchandisers are individuals or teams who visit stores on behalf of your brand, your distributor, or a third-party agency. They are trained in retail compliance, shelf presentation, and the execution of promotions and resets. Depending on your structure, merchandisers may be hired directly by your company, supplied by a distributor, or contracted for specific visits such as launches, promotions, or category resets.

On a day-to-day basis, merchandisers handle the physical work that keeps your brand visible. They restock shelves, rotate inventory to maintain FIFO (First In, First Out), and pull products forward so shelves look full and inviting. They ensure plan-o-gram compliance by checking that your product is placed on the correct shelf, in the correct position, and with the agreed number of facings. When shelves are mis-set or facings disappear, merchandisers correct the issue before it negatively impacts sales.

Merchandisers also play a key role during promotions. They build and maintain secondary displays such as end caps or in-and-out placements, install POS materials, and verify that promotional pricing is showing correctly on shelf and in-store systems. When something isn't executed as agreed, merchandisers report back so issues can be resolved quickly rather than discovered weeks later through declining sales.

Beyond execution, merchandisers act as your eyes and ears in the market. They take photos, monitor competitor activity, flag out-of-stocks, and share insights on pricing, promotions, and shelf conditions. This real-world intelligence helps founders and sales teams understand what's actually happening in stores, not just what was planned.

The importance of merchandising can't be overstated. You're investing in slotting fees, trade spend, promotions, and marketing, and merchandisers protect that investment by making sure it shows up on the shelf. Consistent merchandising maintains shelf presence, prevents lost sales from empty or messy shelves, strengthens relation-ships with retailers, and can drive meaningful sales lift through better facings and execution.

For founders working with limited budgets, merchandising doesn't have to be all or nothing. Many start by hiring part-time reps for top-performing stores, using agencies on a per-visit basis for resets or promotions, or stepping in themselves. In the early days, founders often act as their own merchandisers, visiting stores to face product, check placement, and build rapport with store staff. While not glamorous, this hands-on approach often pays off in stronger execution, better insights, and faster learning.

Pro Tip: Treat merchandisers as your eyes and ears in the field.

The data, photos, and feedback they provide can shape your promotional strategies, competitive positioning, and buyer conversations.

STORE CHECKS / AUDITS

As you definitely know by now, once your product makes it onto the shelf, the work doesn't stop. One of the most important ongoing responsibilities for a founder is making sure that what was promised on paper is actually happening in-store. Store checks, often called retail audits, are the mechanism for doing exactly that. They ensure your product is present, properly placed, correctly priced, and supported the way the retailer agreed, before small execution issues quietly turn into lost sales or bigger problems.

Store checks are systematic visits to retail locations designed to verify product presence, placement, pricing, and promotional execution. These checks can be conducted by you as the founder, by your internal sales team, by merchandisers, or by third-party audit companies. Regardless of who performs them, the goal is the same: catch issues early, document what's happening on the shelf, and protect your brand's performance.

They matter because execution on the shelf directly impacts velocity. Store checks confirm that you have the correct number of facings outlined in the plan-o-gram and help catch situations where competitors slowly encroach on your space or store staff reset shelves incorrectly. They also play a critical role in inventory management. Out-of-stocks kill momentum and can put your placement at risk, and regular audits allow you to spot low inventory before sales are lost or buyers start asking questions.

Promotional execution is another major reason store checks are essential. Audits help confirm that temporary price reductions, shelf tags, signage, and displays are actually live and working as intended. Many chargebacks and bill-backs stem from promotions that weren't executed correctly at store level. Having photos and documentation from store checks gives you leverage to dispute errors and protect your margins.

Store checks also provide invaluable competitive intelligence. By walking the aisle, you can observe competitor pricing, promotions, packaging changes, display activity, and shelf space allocation. This real-world insight strengthens buyer conversations and helps you position your brand more effectively during reviews or reset discussions.

During a store check, founders or reps typically look for a consistent set of indicators: whether the product is on shelf at all, whether it has the agreed number of facings, whether it's positioned correctly within the set, and whether inventory levels look healthy. Audits also verify that promotions and POS elements are in place and working, and that pricing is accurate at both the shelf and register. Finally, observing what competitors are doing often reveals opportunities or risks that aren't visible in sales reports alone.

There are several ways to conduct store checks depending on your stage and budget. In the early days, founders should absolutely do this themselves. Visiting stores builds relationships with staff, keeps you close to your product's real-world performance, and sharpens your instincts as a retailer-facing brand builder. As you grow, merchandisers are often tasked with regular audits across priority stores, while third-party services, such as Trax or Storesight, can provide photo-based reporting and dashboards at scale. No matter the method, consistent store checks are one of the most effective ways to protect velocity, prevent surprises, and stay in control of your retail execution.

Pro Tip: Always document store checks with photos. Photos provide proof for disputes, data for tracking compliance, and visuals to share with buyers when discussing opportunities or issues.

Real-World Simulation

A small beverage brand discovered during audits that half their promotions weren't being executed across a regional chain. They provided photo proof to the buyer, who not only reimbursed the brand for lost promo spend but also prioritized them in the next seasonal reset.

Pro Tip: Build a store check checklist and use it consistently. Over time, you'll gather a valuable data set that shows patterns, informs negotiations, and protects your trade spend investments.

Our Founders' Journey

Elena - Harbor Harvest Foods
(Spiced Mango Preserves)

Elena approached shopper marketing through storytelling and sensory experience. Her spiced mango preserves already stood out visually, but she quickly realized that many shoppers needed inspiration for how to use the product. She focused heavily on sampling and recipe-driven shelf talkers in specialty stores, pairing her preserves with cheeses, breads, and charcuterie suggestions. Elena also invested in small corrugated displays during holiday periods, helping position the product as both an everyday pantry item and a premium giftable food. Her approach reinforced discovery and encouraged shoppers to imagine the product in their own homes.

Marcus - Summit Sips (Clean
Labeled Sparkling Iced Tea)

Marcus treated shopper marketing as a highly coordinated retail growth strategy. His clean-labeled sparkling iced tea entered competitive grocery sets filled with national beverage brands, so visibility became essential. Marcus invested aggressively in end caps, retailer app promotions, loyalty card features, and Retail Media Network advertising tied directly to major accounts. He also used in-store demos strategically during launch windows to accelerate trial and demonstrate velocity quickly. For Marcus, shopper marketing was deeply tied to performance metrics and retailer expectations.

Danielle - Bountiful Bites (Upcycled Snacks)

Danielle leaned into mission-driven merchandising. Her upcycled snacks resonated strongly with environmentally conscious shoppers, so her shopper marketing focused on education and values-based messaging. Shelf talkers emphasized sustainability benefits, while temporary displays highlighted food waste reduction in a way that felt approachable rather than overly technical. Danielle also partnered with select retailers on Earth Month promotions and digital campaigns tied to sustainability initiatives. Her success came from making the product feel both purposeful and accessible.

Andre - Kindred Grains
(Ancient Grain Snacks)

Andre approached shopper marketing with discipline and restraint. Rather than spreading his budget across too many programs, he focused on a few high-impact tactics. His ancient grain snacks performed well when paired with strong shelf signage and targeted sampling in health-focused retailers. Andre also invested early in a store locator platform after realizing that awareness without easy product access was limiting conversion. His approach reflected a broader philosophy: every shopper marketing dollar needed a clear objective and measurable outcome.

CHAPTER FIVE

Consumer Marketing and Promotion

Throughout my years developing marketing campaigns for global brands, one truth became clear: consumers don't just buy what you make, they buy what you *mean.*

No matter how innovative your product is, if consumers don't understand who you are or why you exist, they'll walk right past it. In the crowded world of packaged food and beverage, marketing isn't about shouting louder; it's about connecting more deeply.

I've worked across the spectrum, from negotiating national advertising budgets to helping startup founders design grassroots sampling programs. What separates brands that grow from those that stall isn't always the size of their spend, a lot falls on the clarity of their message and the consistency of their execution.

This chapter will help you understand how to transform your brand from a product on a shelf into a story people want to be part of. We'll explore the psychology behind purchasing decisions, the tactics that drive trial and repeat sales, and how to build campaigns that feel authentic, because in today's market, authenticity is the ultimate currency.

ATL vs. BTL (Above the
Line vs. Below the Line)

As a brand matures, conversations about marketing investment begin to take on a more structured vocabulary. Two of the most common classifications are ATL and BTL, shorthand for above the line and below the line. These frameworks help teams, buyers, and investors understand whether dollars are being used to create broad awareness or to drive targeted action. Knowing the difference makes it easier to justify budgets and align expectations around results.

Above the line activity refers to mass reach initiatives intended to put your name in front of as many people as possible. Think traditional and large scale media such as television, radio, print, outdoor, or wide digital display networks. These efforts are powerful for visibility and brand building, yet they are typically less precise when it comes to measuring immediate sales impact. A commercial during a popular cooking program, a billboard close to major shopping corridors, or banner ads across lifestyle sites can dramatically increase recognition, but they require meaningful investment and usually make sense once distribution is strong enough to capture the demand they generate.

Below the line programs are more targeted and performance oriented. They are designed to influence specific audiences and are usually easier to tie directly to conversion. Sampling events, retailer loyalty discounts, email campaigns to direct customers, or partnerships with influencers who speak to a defined community fall into this bucket. For emerging companies, this approach is often more practical because budgets are tighter and proof of return is critical. BTL activity allows a founder to test, learn, and demonstrate velocity without betting the farm on national awareness.

The distinction matters because stakeholders listen for it. Retail partners want to know how traffic will be driven to their stores, while investors want evidence that spending is disciplined and aligned with growth. When leaders show they understand when to build reach and when to drive conversion, it signals strategic clarity. The most effective plans rarely rely on one or the other, they evolve, starting with targeted activation and gradually layering in broader awareness as distribution expands.

Pro Tip: For most startups, BTL should dominate the budget early on. Save ATL activities (like TV or large-scale billboards) until you have broader distribution and the resources to sustain them.

The Consumer Journey

Securing distribution is an achievement, yet it is only the opening move. Sustainable growth depends on guiding people from discovery to repeat purchase. That progression is the consumer journey, a practical framework that explains how someone moves from noticing a brand to actively choosing it again. For food and beverage CPG companies, the journey is often viewed through four connected stages: awareness, relevance, acceptance, and preference.

Awareness is the introduction. This is the moment a consumer first realizes the brand exists. It can happen through digital media, influencer mentions, press coverage, or simply catching sight of the product in a busy aisle. Without visibility, trial is impossible, because no one can buy what they have never encountered. Early on, smart brands concentrate their resources on the audience most likely to respond rather than attempting to reach everyone at once.

Relevance answers the next question in the shopper's mind, why this product matters to them. Here, packaging, claims, and placement work together to signal fit. Nutritional benefits, lifestyle alignment, cultural cues, or convenience all help a consumer quickly determine whether the item belongs in their basket. Recognition alone will not move inventory, the product must feel like a solution.

Acceptance is the conversion point, the instant curiosity turns into action. A shopper places the item in the cart, scans it at checkout, or taps purchase online. Promotions, sampling, compelling design, strong reviews, and favorable shelf position all reduce hesitation. This is the leap from knowing about a brand to experiencing it, and it is where many young companies either gain momentum or stall.

Preference is the long game. After trial, the consumer decides whether the experience justified the choice. Consistent quality, emotional connection, and reinforcement through ongoing engagement transform a one time buyer into a repeat purchaser. When preference takes hold, people seek out the brand, recommend it, and often pay full price without prompting. That loyalty fuels predictable revenue and provides the foundation for expansion.

Each stage builds on the one before it. Visibility opens the door, meaning creates interest, trial delivers proof, and satisfaction earns devotion. Brands that deliberately support consumers at every step are the ones that move from shelf presence to household name.

Awareness

What It Is:

The stage where consumers first discover that your brand exists. Awareness is about visibility, making sure your target shopper knows your product is out there.

How It's Built:

- **Digital advertising** (social media ads, search, influencer campaigns).

- **In-store visibility** (end caps, shelf talkers, demos).

- **PR and earned media** (press mentions, food blogs, podcasts).

- **Word of mouth** (recommendations from friends, family, or store staff).

Why It Matters:

Without awareness, nothing else happens. Consumers can't try or buy a product they don't know exists. For founders, the challenge is to cut through the noise of thousands of SKUs in-store.

Pro Tip: Focus early awareness efforts on your most likely shoppers (existing category users) rather than trying to reach everyone.

Awareness: Do they know you exist?

At this stage, the goal is simple: get your brand in front of your *ideal* consumer. It's also good to understand who the existing category consumers are…who currently buys your competition.

Touchpoints that drive awareness:

- Organic and paid social media

- Sampling (in-store, events, DTC sample packs)

- Farmers markets and pop-up events

- Influencer mentions and recommendations

- PR features in lifestyle or food publications
-
- Content that speaks to pain points or desires

Figure: Awareness

Relevance

What It Is:

Once consumers know your product exists, the next hurdle is answering the question: *"Why should I care?"* Relevance is about connecting your product to the consumer's needs, values, or lifestyle.

How It's Built:

- Clear packaging that communicates benefits (organic, gluten-free, high-protein).

- Messaging that resonates with your target audience's values (sustainability, convenience, indulgence).

- Placement in the right channel (ex., health-conscious products in natural retailers, indulgent snacks in convenience).

. . .

Why It Matters:

Awareness without relevance won't drive trial. If your product doesn't feel like a solution to the consumer's needs, they'll pass it by.

Pro Tip: Relevance requires focus. Don't try to be everything to everyone, define your target consumer and speak directly to them.

Relevance: Do they believe your product fits their needs?

Once someone becomes aware of your product, the next hurdle is getting them to believe it's for them. This is where your product's positioning, messaging, and visual branding matter most. Relevance gets consumers to trial, the moment where they decide to try and purchase.

Touchpoints that drive relevance:

- Sampling (in-store, events, DTC sample packs)

- Retail promotions (BOGO, coupons, discounts)

- Low-barrier formats (single serves or trial sizes)

- Reviews and testimonials

- Transparent and honest packaging (benefits, certifications)

- Targeted email marketing

- Storytelling through brand origin or founder story

- Educational content (ex., how it fits their diet, how to use it)

Figure: Relevance

Acceptance

What It Is:

The stage where the consumer decides to give your product a chance and actually makes a purchase. Acceptance is trial, the moment someone picks your product off the shelf or clicks "buy."

. . .

How It's Built:

- **Price promotions** (BOGOs, coupons, loyalty card discounts).

- **In-store demos** and sampling ("taste the difference" moments).

- **Strong packaging design** that catches attention and builds trust.

- **Retail placement** (eye-level, multiple facings, secondary locations).

Why It Matters:

Trial is the critical inflection point. Without it, your brand remains a name consumers recognize but never experience. Acceptance is the bridge between curiosity and loyalty.

Pro Tip: Lower the barrier to trial, whether through price, sampling, or distribution. Make it easy for consumers to say "yes" the first time.

Acceptance: They tried it and like it!

If you've made it this far, congratulations, you've earned enough trust to trigger interest. Now, you need to convert that interest into trial.

Touchpoints that drive acceptance (trial):

- Insider programs (advance access to product drops, events)
- Retail promotions (BOGO, discounts)
- Reviews and testimonials

Figure: Acceptance

Preference

What It Is:

The ultimate goal: the consumer doesn't just buy your product once, they choose it again and again, even when competitors are on the shelf. Preference is loyalty.

How It's Built:

- Delivering consistently high quality.

- Meeting or exceeding expectations after trial.

- Building emotional connection through storytelling and values alignment.

- Reinforcing the relationship with consumer promotions, loyalty programs, and brand community-building.

Why It Matters:

Preference is where **r**epeat purchases happen, the driver of sustainable growth and long-term profitability. Preference also creates brand advocates: loyal customers who recommend your product to others.

Pro Tip: The biggest test of preference is whether consumers are willing to pay full price for your product once promotions end.

Preference: They love you and they love to tell others!

Once someone tries your product, they're evaluating it across several dimensions: taste, texture, packaging, price, and emotional connection. If you deliver, they may buy again. If you delight, they may become *loyalists* and even advocates.

Touchpoints that drive preference:

- Featuring top fans on social
- Priority updates (new product launches, events, promotions)
- Consumer surveys, suggestions, and feedback
- Merchandise

Figure: Preference

BONUS - UNDERSTANDING CURRENT CATEGORY USERS

Before a single case ships, a founder needs clarity on the people who are already buying within the aisle they plan to enter. Every category comes with established routines, loyalties, price expectations, and emotional triggers. When entrepreneurs become overly attached to their own idea, it is easy to overlook the fact that shoppers are not starting from zero. Studying current buyers of chips, bars, frozen entrées, or beverages reveals how decisions are actually made, where frustrations live, and which needs remain underserved. That understanding allows a brand to position itself intelligently instead of trying to persuade the wrong audience to behave differently.

This perspective delivers several essential advantages. It clarifies who is purchasing, what problem the category is solving for them, and where genuine whitespace may exist. Without that groundwork, even beautiful packaging or breakthrough formulation can land flat. A product designed for wellness seekers may struggle if most shoppers are motivated by comfort or indulgence. A premium strategy may fail in an aisle dominated by value. Insight into the existing consumer base helps ensure that innovation connects with reality.

Building this picture requires looking at multiple layers. Demographic information such as age, income, geography, and household composition identifies who is in the market, but it does not explain motivation. Psychographics go further, uncovering attitudes about health, convenience, sustainability, or taste, and revealing whether buyers are loyalists or experimenters. Behavioral data then shows how those beliefs translate into action, which stores they visit, how frequently they purchase, what else goes into the basket, and how easily they switch brands. Together, these lenses transform assumptions into strategy and give founders a far stronger chance of entering the shelf with relevance and precision.

What's In It For the Consumer

Every product fulfills a "job" for the consumer, solving a problem, satisfying a craving, or fulfilling an emotional need. Understanding the *job* that current category users hire your product to do gives you clarity on your competitive positioning.

For example:

- **Cold brew coffee** isn't just about caffeine; it's about *energy, sophistication, and convenience.*

- **Protein snacks** aren't just about nutrition; they're about *control, self-care, and performance.*

- **Frozen meals** aren't just about convenience; they're about *reducing decision fatigue* after a long day.

The better you understand the *why* behind category purchases, the more powerfully you can align your brand narrative with the real human needs driving them.

Figure: What's In It For the Consumer

How to Learn About Your Category Users

Syndicated Data: Nielsen, Circana (formerly IRI), SPINS

These platforms offer quantitative insights on sales velocity, share of category, and household penetration by brand. While costly, they're invaluable for understanding category dynamics and user demographics at scale.

Retailer Insights

Retail buyers often have access to consumer panel data specific to their stores. When pitching, ask questions like:

"Who is your primary shopper in this category?"

"Which attributes, flavor, price, or claims, are most important to your customers here?"

Retailers appreciate when founders ask thoughtful, data-informed questions rather than relying solely on assumptions.

Social Listening and Online Communities

Reddit threads, Facebook groups, and TikTok trends can be gold mines of qualitative insight. Observe what consumers are saying about current products in your category, their pain points, preferences, and emotional language.

Surveys and Taste Panels

You don't need a massive budget to gather honest feedback. Conduct small-scale surveys, host focus groups, or set up taste tests at farmers markets to hear firsthand how consumers perceive your product versus existing options.

Consumer Psychology
in Food Marketing

Food marketing succeeds when it starts with human behavior rather than persuasion. Every trip down the aisle is shaped by instinct, memory, and feeling just as much as price tags or promotions. Meals and snacks carry meaning, they connect people to heritage, family rituals, aspirations about wellness, and moments of reward. When someone chooses a brand, the decision is rarely a purely rational comparison. It is a small emotional affirmation. Companies that understand this dynamic design products and messages that resonate far beyond functional benefits.

A large share of purchasing happens on autopilot. Shoppers rely on shortcuts built from past experiences, sensory cues, and personal identity. Certain forces appear again and again. Comfort and nostalgia make familiar flavors feel safe. Health and control appeal to people trying to manage busy or uncertain lives. Discovery introduces novelty and conversation. Identity allows food to signal who someone is, or hopes to be. Indulgence provides permission to enjoy a treat without abandoning broader goals. The most durable brands pick the emotional territories they can authentically own and reinforce them at every touchpoint, from pack design to social presence to in-store activity.

Because food engages the body so completely, sensory signals become powerful brand assets. Visual language sets expectations before an item is ever picked up. Aromas can unlock memory faster than any advertisement. Flavor becomes a signature that either reassures or surprises. The weight and finish of packaging quietly communicate quality. Even sound, the snap of a seal or the crunch of a bite, can confirm freshness and satisfaction. When these elements align, the experience feels cohesive and trustworthy. That consistency is what transforms a single purchase into habit, and habit into loyalty.

The Psychology of Packaging and Perception

Packaging is your *first salesperson*. Consumers often make their purchase decision in under seven seconds, and your design must instantly convey trust, quality, and relevance.

- **Color Psychology:**

    ○ Green = health, freshness, sustainability

    ○ Red = energy, appetite stimulation

    ○ Black/Gold = luxury, indulgence

    ○ White/Neutral = purity, simplicity

- **Cognitive Fluency:** The easier your packaging is to understand, the faster consumers will connect with it. Overly busy designs or unclear claims create friction and doubt.

- **Social Proof:** Awards, certifications, and endorsements serve as psychological shortcuts, signaling to buyers that they're making a good choice.

A great package doesn't just *contain* your product, it communicates your promise before a word is spoken.

Figure: The Psychology of Packaging and Perception

Behavioral Triggers in Food Shopping

Understanding consumer behavior in retail environments is just as important as understanding emotion.

- **Impulse Zones:** Endcaps, checkout lanes, and eye-level shelves are designed to capture emotional, last-minute decisions.

- **Price Perception:** Round prices ($5.00) suggest premium quality; prices ending in 9 ($4.99) suggest value.

- **Scarcity and Urgency:** Limited-time offers and seasonal SKUs activate fear of missing out (FOMO).

- **Anchoring:** When a higher-priced product sits next to a mid-tier item, the mid-tier suddenly feels more affordable.

- **Loyalty Loops:** Once consumers trust a brand, they default to it automatically, reducing the mental load of choosing.

Knowing how shoppers think in-store helps you position your brand and promotions more effectively.

The Role of Storytelling in Consumer Psychology

Great brands understand that meaning travels farther than ingredients. When a company communicates its origins, its mission, or the people behind it, the product becomes more than something to eat. Narrative creates emotional framing. It helps shoppers understand why a brand exists and why it deserves space in their lives. A founder's journey, a connection to heritage, a commitment to craft or community, all of these elements turn a transaction into a relationship. When people see themselves reflected in that narrative, purchasing begins to feel personal. They are not simply choosing an item, they are participating in something larger.

Applying psychology in this way is less about persuasion and more about attunement. The essential questions become practical. What need is being met, comfort, energy, discovery, reassurance? What impression forms the moment someone sees the package? Does the price communicate accessibility or exclusivity in a way that matches the promise? How might sampling, digital content, or in-store activity engage sight, taste, texture, even memory? When these choices line up, the brand experience feels coherent.

Storytelling and Brand Narrative

Exceptional products rarely move on attributes alone. What persuades both trade partners and shoppers is a grounded explanation of who you are, what you produce, and why it deserves attention. Your narrative is your infrastructure. It influences how you are positioned, how much you can charge, how buyers perceive risk, how talent evaluates you, and how investors assess durability. Specific, lived details are what create credibility. The imperfect first batches, the family influence, the early mistakes, the tiny kitchen, these elements transform a brand from abstract to human, and from human to trustworthy.

Why Story Matters

A defensible narrative is one of the few assets competitors cannot easily replicate. Ingredients can be matched, claims can be reformulated, packaging can be refreshed. Your lived history cannot. Concrete specificity builds belief. When buyers and shoppers hear real places, real constraints, real decisions, skepticism softens. Strong storytelling also supports price integrity because people understand what they are paying for beyond the product itself. Internally, it aligns teams and partners around a shared direction, ensuring that sales, marketing, and operations are reinforcing the same promise. At shelf, it becomes the bridge between emotion and logic, giving consumers a feeling first and a justification second. If the message feels overly polished or universally interchangeable, it will likely fade into the background.

The Building Blocks of a Brand Narrative

Effective narratives are solid. They can travel from a buyer meeting to a trade show booth to packaging copy without losing shape. Most are built from a clear origin moment, the problem that needed solving, a point of difference that can be defended, proof that validates the claim, the impact on the customer, a view of where the company is headed next, and a simple next step for the listener. Each component should be concise. Depth lives in supporting materials. Your first impression should be tight, memorable, and repeatable.

Narrative Archetypes That Work
in Food and Beverage CPG

Patterns tend to repeat across winning brands. Some succeed by emphasizing culinary lineage and craft. Others rally around ingredient transparency or removal of unwanted elements. Functional benefit stories rooted in performance or science resonate strongly in many modern categories. Environmental leadership, time savings, or waste reduction can also anchor a compelling frame. The discipline is choosing a primary identity and, at most, one supporting layer. When everything is emphasized, nothing is retained.

Customer as Hero

The most persuasive narratives shift the spotlight away from the company and toward the person being served. The shopper discovers something new, recognizes that it fits their life, tries it with confidence, and ultimately returns because it consistently solves a need. In trade conversations, the hero becomes the category itself. The brand's role is to recruit new households, add incremental purchases, and strengthen overall performance. When framed this way, the partnership becomes obvious.

Message Architecture

To keep communication aligned, many strong organizations codify their narrative into a simple framework. At the top sits a single umbrella promise. Beneath it are a small number of pillars that define what the brand stands for, followed by tangible evidence that proves those pillars are real. From there, language can flex depending on the audience. Shoppers may hear about flavor and ease, buyers about margin and growth, investors about scale and efficiency. The spine remains intact even as emphasis shifts.

Voice and Tone Guidelines

Repetition builds memory. Selecting a handful of tonal attributes provides guardrails for everyone who speaks on behalf of the brand. Concrete verbs, observable process, and measurable statements strengthen authority. Vague claims, borrowed identities, and exaggerated language weaken it. Many companies benefit from defining not only preferred expressions but also phrases they intentionally avoid, particularly those that create regulatory exposure or undermine seriousness.

Authenticity Checklist

A simple internal test can protect narrative strength. If a competitor could make the same statement without changing a word, it is too generic. Strong claims usually include time, place, method, or constraint. Evidence should appear quickly, not after prolonged explanation. The tension being solved must be real, not cosmetic. Finally, what is said must align with what is printed, certified, and legally supportable. Consistency between story and reality is what sustains trust over time.

Your Brand's Digital Presence

In the modern marketplace, online visibility often shapes perception before a product is ever touched, tasted, or stocked. Buyers vet credibility digitally. Consumers confirm trust digitally. Investors gauge momentum digitally. A cohesive footprint across owned and earned channels signals seriousness, operational maturity, and market readiness. Weak or inconsistent presence raises immediate questions. Strong presence shortens sales cycles.

Website

Your site functions as the brand's headquarters. It is the place buyers confirm professionalism, where media verify facts, and where consumers seek reassurance before purchase. Clear product detail, strong imagery, and easy navigation remove friction and build confidence. Essential elements include a compelling company story, complete product pages with ingredients and nutrition information, and a direct path to purchase or retail discovery. Because most traffic now originates on phones, performance on mobile is not optional, it is foundational.

Social Media

Social platforms are the living expression of your brand. They demonstrate energy, responsiveness, and proof that real people care. Retail partners routinely review feeds to assess whether a company can support sell-through. Consumers look for cues of popularity and authenticity. Visual channels are ideal for appetite appeal, preparation ideas, and community engagement, while professional networks provide access to decision-makers and potential partners. Consistency in voice, design language, and posting rhythm reinforces reliability.

Press

Third-party validation carries a weight that paid messaging cannot replicate. When journalists, editors, or hosts choose to feature a product, they lend borrowed authority. That endorsement can influence buyers evaluating risk and shoppers seeking reassurance. Housing coverage in a dedicated press area, supported by photography, fact sheets, and contact information, makes it easier for new media opportunities to emerge and for partners to verify your reputation.

Store Locator

A locator connects curiosity to commerce. Once someone decides they want the product, speed and clarity determine whether the purchase actually happens. Accurate listings protect trust, while integrated online purchase links accommodate different shopping preferences. Over time, search data from locator activity becomes a strategic asset, revealing geographic pockets of demand that can inform future distribution conversations.

Influencers

Creators can extend reach into communities that traditional marketing struggles to access. Their value lies not simply in audience size but in credibility with that audience. Partnerships work best when alignment feels natural and enthusiasm is genuine. Smaller creators frequently generate stronger engagement and more efficient economics, particularly for young brands building early loyalty. Measuring success requires attention to response and conversion, not vanity metrics.

Blogs

Long-form content provides depth that quick posts cannot. It allows you to educate, inspire, and answer the questions buyers and consumers are already asking search engines. Over time, this builds discoverability and authority within your category. Topics might include usage ideas, sourcing practices, or broader conversations connected to your mission. When distributed across email and social channels, each article becomes a renewable marketing asset.

Key Takeaway

Your digital presence should work as a cohesive ecosystem. A buyer reads about you in a trade publication, checks your website, and then sees active social content. A consumer finds you on Instagram, clicks through to your store locator, and buys at their local grocer. Each channel reinforces the other, and together they build the credibility and accessibility your brand needs to thrive.

BRAND VOICE AND CONSISTENCY ACROSS CHANNELS

Your brand voice is all about the emotional signature behind every communication touchpoint. It shapes how people interpret your intentions, your professionalism, and your reliability. In a world where shoppers may meet your company on a shelf, on a phone, in an email, and through a retailer's promotion, cohesion becomes proof of maturity. Variation for the sake of novelty can feel creative internally, yet externally it often reads as uncertainty. A strong voice feels like a familiar person, recognizable wherever the conversation begins.

Defining Your Brand Voice

Think of voice as personality translated into language. It should echo mission, values, and the role your product plays in someone's life. Some brands communicate with authority and expertise, others with warmth and humor, others with calm reassurance. The goal is not to sound impressive, it is to sound unmistakable. When the voice aligns with the expectations of the target consumer, communication becomes intuitive rather than forced.

Voice vs. Tone: The Subtle but Critical Difference

Voice remains stable. Tone flexes with circumstance. A company that is consistently knowledgeable and approachable may still shift expression depending on the moment. A recall notice requires clarity and empathy, while a launch announcement can feel energetic and celebratory. The underlying personality never changes, yet the delivery respects context. Brands that master this distinction feel human and trustworthy.

The Role of Consistency Across Channels

Recognition precedes trust, and trust precedes purchase. Because consumers experience brands as a collection of touchpoints rather than isolated messages, alignment across platforms is essential. Your language on pack should sound connected to your website. Your social captions should feel related to your emails. Your retail materials should reinforce what shoppers have already heard elsewhere.

When these pieces harmonize, the brand becomes easier to remember and easier to choose.

Packaging

For many shoppers, the first encounter happens in the aisle. The words on the package act as an introduction and must immediately reflect personality. Whether the approach is playful, refined, technical, or heritage-driven, the tone should feel continuous with everything a customer might later read online or hear from a sales representative.

Website and E-Commerce

Online environments deepen the relationship. Headlines, product descriptions, and company narratives should extend the same identity introduced on shelf. When the digital experience sounds disconnected from the packaging, confidence erodes. Continuity reassures visitors that the operation behind the brand is stable and intentional.

Social Media

Here the personality breathes in real time. Conversation, responsiveness, and community expression show dimension, yet the character must remain familiar. Platforms may encourage slightly different energy levels, but the audience should still recognize who is speaking without checking the profile name.

Email and Direct Messaging

Inbox communication carries a sense of privilege. The brand has been invited into personal space. Language should therefore feel considerate and appreciative while maintaining its established character. Done well, this balance strengthens loyalty and repeat purchase behavior.

Retail and In-Store Marketing

Materials seen in stores should echo the same identity consumers recognize elsewhere. Alignment between digital storytelling and physical execution reinforces authenticity and assures retailers that the brand can support sell-through with coherent messaging.

Why Consistency Matters

Cohesion reduces friction in decision-making. It helps people feel familiar with the company, even after brief exposure. A steady voice increases recall, allowing shoppers to recognize communication without always needing visual cues. It ensures that each interaction reinforces the central narrative rather than competing with it. Internally, it also accelerates content development, giving teams and partners a clear framework for how the brand should sound.

Consistency is not sameness. Messages will evolve. Campaigns will change. What endures is the personality guiding them, steady, reliable, and easy to recognize.

Building Your Brand Voice Guide

Every brand should document its communication style in a Brand Voice Guide, a simple, one- to two-page reference for internal and external partners.

Include:

- **Voice Attributes:** 3–5 defining traits (ex., "Warm, Confident, Thoughtful, Approachable, Expert").

- **Do/Don't Examples:** How your brand would and wouldn't phrase things.

- **Tone Adjustments by Channel:** How your voice adapts for different platforms.

- **Sample Copy Blocks:** Packaging blurbs, captions, and product descriptions written in your brand voice.

This guide ensures that everyone, from copywriters to sales reps, communicates with the same personality and purpose.

Pro Tip: Consistency Doesn't Mean Sameness

You can keep your voice consistent while tailoring your message for the moment.

For example, a natural beverage brand might sound:

- **Playful** on social media ("Hydrate happy!")

- **Professional** in retail sell sheets ("Made with naturally sourced electrolytes")

- **Personal** in emails ("Hey, you're one of our favorite sippers—thanks for staying refreshed with us.")

The tone shifts, but the essence, the warmth, wit, and confidence, remain unchanged.

Pull vs. Push Communications

How a company speaks to the market can determine how efficiently it grows. Some efforts broadcast messages outward in order to capture attention quickly. Others create gravity, encouraging people to come closer on their own. Both approaches are necessary. One accelerates discovery, the other builds attachment. The art is knowing when to apply pressure and when to cultivate attraction.

Push Communications

Push activity begins with the brand. It places a message directly in front of an audience, often interrupting whatever they were doing to introduce an offer, an announcement, or a call to act. Because of this, push tactics are usually paid, highly visible, and engineered for reach. They are powerful when speed matters, such as launching into a new retailer, supporting a promotion, or entering a competitive window where attention is scarce.

Examples typically include digital advertising, retail circular features, end-cap programs, outbound emails, and formal announcements distributed to media. The advantage is immediacy and control. A campaign can be turned on, targeted, and scaled with precision. The challenge is sustainability. Once spending stops, visibility often fades, and excessive repetition can create fatigue.

Pull Communications

Pull activity starts with the consumer. Instead of interrupting, it attracts. Interest grows because the audience finds value, relevance, or inspiration in what the brand provides. Over time this creates familiarity, then trust, and eventually loyalty. Pull strategies are frequently rooted in education, storytelling, and utility rather than overt persuasion.

This can take the form of discoverable website content, community engagement on social platforms, earned media mentions, referrals, and tools that help shoppers find or understand the product more easily. The benefit is durability. Momentum compounds and credibility strengthens. The tradeoff is time. Pull rarely produces instant spikes, it rewards patience and consistency.

Why Both Matter

Short-term traction and long-term equity are built differently. Broadcasting messages can drive trial and help win distribution, while attraction ensures shoppers return without needing constant incentives. Retail partners and financial backers look for evidence of both capabilities. They want to see a company that can create bursts of demand when needed and nurture a relationship that sustains performance after the spotlight moves elsewhere.

When these forces operate together, awareness converts to habit. The brand becomes not only visible, but wanted.

Real-World Example

A plant-based yogurt brand might push with Instagram ads and retailer coupons during launch, but simultaneously pull through recipe content, sustainability storytelling, and influencer partnerships that make consumers want to seek them out beyond the promo.

Don't lean exclusively on push, constant discounts and ads will erode margins. Balance it with pull strategies that create authentic demand and strengthen your brand story.

Pro Tip: Ask yourself before every campaign: *"Am I pushing this product into the market, or am I pulling consumers toward me? And do I have a healthy mix of both?"*

Community Building and
Brand Ambassadors

In packaged food and beverage, influence travels fastest through people. Long before an ad converts or an algorithm amplifies, trust is formed in conversations between friends, families, and peers. Brands that endure understand this. They cultivate real relationships that turn buyers into believers and believers into advocates.

Community is not a vanity metric. It is not follower count or impressions. It is connection, recognition, and shared meaning. When shoppers feel they are part of something, they stay longer, purchase more often, and invite others in.

Why Community Matters

Food is naturally communal. It is tied to ritual, celebration, identity, and memory. When a brand successfully gathers people around an idea, it moves beyond transaction and becomes participation. That shift changes everything about resilience and growth.

A committed community can spark organic word of mouth, deepen repeat purchase behavior, offer immediate feedback on innovation, and create authentic content that no studio can manufacture. During competitive or economic pressure, that emotional loyalty becomes insulation. The people who feel connected remain.

The relationships invested in today become tomorrow's most efficient marketing engine.

Building Community from the Ground Up

Strong communities rarely appear overnight. They are built deliberately by understanding who your audience is and what matters in their lives beyond your product.

Define your shared purpose.

Every durable group rallies around belief. The item you sell may be simple, but the meaning can be larger, making better choices easier, celebrating heritage, supporting active lifestyles, or bringing joy back to weeknight meals. Purpose gives people a reason to gather.

Choose gathering spaces.

Connection should happen where participation feels natural. That may be digital platforms, local events, retail activations, or intimate newsletters. The medium matters less than whether people feel welcomed and recognized.

Engage in real dialogue.

Answer comments. Thank customers. Spotlight their creativity. Ask questions and respond to what you hear. Audiences can sense when interaction is automated or extractive. They remain where it feels human.

The Role of Brand Ambassadors

Ambassadors extend your reach through credibility. They are not simply content creators. They are individuals whose lives already align with what you represent, and whose enthusiasm would exist even without compensation.

Because they are trusted within their own circles, their advocacy carries weight. Their recommendations feel like advice, not advertising. Over time they become connective tissue between your company and the culture surrounding it.

Building an Ambassador Program

The strongest initiatives begin close to home. Identify early supporters, loyal shoppers, chefs, trainers, or organizers who already believe. Invite them into deeper participation before pursuing scale.

Offer access, not just product. Early tastings, behind-the-scenes updates, branded experiences, and communication with your team create belonging. Provide clarity on expectations so representation stays aligned, while leaving space for personal voice. Authenticity travels further than scripts.

Measurement is important, engagement, referrals, retail impact, but so is recognition. Celebrate contributions publicly. Make ambassadors proud of the role they play in your growth.

Community Over Influence

Reach can be rented. Relationships must be earned. A famous endorsement may deliver attention for a moment, but a network of genuine supporters sustains credibility for years.

Today's consumers want connection with brands that listen, reflect their values, and participate in the world with integrity. When that connection is real, promotion becomes conversation, and conversation becomes loyalty.

Campaigns

Promotions matter, but real momentum comes from coordinated efforts built around a clear objective and timeframe. A campaign unifies digital, retail, PR, social, and shopper activity so each touchpoint reinforces the same message. Rather than scattered tactics, you create a focused chapter in your brand story with a beginning, middle, and measurable end.

Awareness Campaigns

Awareness campaigns concentrate on introduction and recognition. The aim is to ensure the right audience knows you exist and understands why you are different. These programs typically blend reach with narrative through social content, creator partnerships, earned media, events, or sponsorships. Repetition builds familiarity, familiarity builds confidence, and confidence opens the door to trial. Without awareness, even the strongest product remains invisible.

Sales Campaigns

Sales campaigns are designed to trigger action. Here the goal is urgency, motivating shoppers to buy within a defined window. Retail promotions, digital offers, limited time pricing, bundles, and geo targeted support work together to convert interest into movement. When executed well, these programs drive the velocity buyers expect and create proof that your brand can turn attention into revenue.

The strongest strategies connect both approaches. Awareness fills the pipeline with future customers, sales converts them. Overreliance on visibility can create curiosity without purchase, while constant discounting may spark spikes but weaken long term equity. Brands that grow sustainably plan rhythms where storytelling and conversion strengthen each other.

Success depends on defining outcomes before launch. Whether the metric is impressions, engagement, trial, repeat purchase, or incremental dollars, clarity enables smarter decisions and better performance the next time. Done right, campaigns deliver not just results, but learning and a repeatable engine for growth.

Coupons

Price incentives remain one of the most reliable ways to spark trial in food retail. A well designed offer gives shoppers a simple nudge to choose your item today instead of postponing the decision. For founders, coupons are not merely discounts, they are strategic levers that influence velocity, buyer confidence, and repeat purchase patterns. When deployed thoughtfully, they can introduce new households to your brand while still protecting long term pricing power.

There are several primary formats, each serving a different objective.

Manufacturer Coupons

Manufacturer coupons are issued by the brand and can be redeemed wherever the product is sold. They provide broad reach and are useful when building awareness across multiple accounts at once. Because reimbursement comes from the supplier, these programs travel well across regions and channels, especially when paired with national PR or digital activity.

. . .

On-Pack Instant Redeemable Coupons (IRCs)

On pack instant redeemables, often called IRCs or peelies, work at the most decisive moment, right at the shelf. The value is visible, immediate, and effortless, which makes them particularly effective for launches or line extensions where hesitation might otherwise prevent trial. They convert consideration into action without requiring shoppers to search, print, or remember anything later.

Retailer Specific Coupons

Retailer specific coupons are created in partnership with an individual chain and are valid only in that banner. Buyers appreciate exclusivity because it drives traffic and strengthens loyalty to their stores. These programs often appear in circulars, apps, or end cap features and can support deeper collaboration with priority accounts, though the trade off is narrower reach.

Digital Coupons

Digital platforms such as rebate and activation apps extend offers directly to mobile first consumers. These programs are attractive for growing brands because they allow precise geographic or demographic targeting and provide clear redemption data. The analytics can help demonstrate incrementality, profile new users, and refine future campaigns with more confidence.

Loyalty Program Coupons

Loyalty program coupons harness a retailer's own shopper intelligence. Discounts are applied automatically when customers scan their card or phone, making the experience frictionless. Because retailers can link redemptions to purchase history, these promotions often resonate strongly with buyers who want proof that incentives are attracting the right households.

Across all formats, the principle is the same. Lower the risk of first purchase, gather evidence of demand, and convert curiosity into repeat behavior. Used with discipline, coupons become more than a temporary price cut. They are investments in household penetration, relationships with retail partners, and the long arc of brand growth.

Key Takeaway

Coupons come in many forms, but their purpose is the same: reduce trial risk for the shopper while driving velocities for your brand. The most effective coupon strategy combines multiple types: on-pack for impulse, retailer-specific for partnerships, and digital for precise targeting.

Pro Tip: Always track redemption rates and lift in velocities. A coupon's success isn't just about how many people used it, it's about how many came back and bought again at full price.

COUPON DEVELOPMENT AND CLEARINGHOUSES

Creating an offer involves far more than placing a dollar amount on a piece of paper or loading a code into an app. Behind every redemption sits an operational system that determines how the incentive is structured, how it reaches shoppers, and how money flows back to the retailer. When founders understand this infrastructure, they can run promotions that are both effective at shelf and financially controlled.

Coupon development begins with defining the mechanics of the offer. The value must be compelling enough to motivate action while still protecting margin. Decisions follow about format, whether the incentive will live on packaging, circulate digitally, or exist exclusively with a retail partner. Restrictions such as eligible items, minimum quantities, and expiration dates clarify intent and prevent misuse. Once the mechanics are set, design becomes critical. Clear hierarchy, legible copy, and strong brand cues improve trust and redemption, while clutter or ambiguity creates hesitation. Distribution planning then determines how shoppers will encounter the offer, perhaps through mail, at shelf, through retailer apps, or across third party digital platforms. Finally, technical tracking elements such as standardized barcodes allow every redemption to be traced, audited, and analyzed later. In practice, these instruments function like money, and they deserve the same rigor, controls, and documentation.

After shoppers redeem, clearinghouses step in to reconcile the transaction. These third party partners receive physical or digital submissions from retailers, validate authenticity, aggregate totals, and bill the manufacturer. Once payment is collected, funds are returned to the retailer, closing the financial loop. Their scale allows millions of coupons to be processed accurately while also flagging irregularities that might indicate fraud or operational errors. Detailed reporting from clearinghouses gives brands visibility into redemption rates, geographic performance, and timing, insights that can shape future promotional strategy.

Costs accompany every stage, from creative development and printing to per piece processing charges. While digital formats often lower risk, safeguards remain necessary in any medium. The discipline applied here determines whether a coupon becomes a smart growth investment or an uncontrolled expense. When managed carefully, the system delivers something invaluable, verified proof that shoppers responded to your invitation to try.

Real-World Example

A granola bar startup launches a $1 off manufacturer coupon distributed via a digital platform. Consumers redeem at multiple grocery chains. The clearinghouse collects all redemptions, verifies them, and sends the brand a report:

- 18,000 coupons redeemed
- Redemption rate: 12%

- Net reimbursement to retailers: $18,000 + clearinghouse fees

This gives the brand both accountability and insights into consumer behavior.

If you plan to run coupon campaigns at scale, partner with an experienced clearinghouse early. This protects you from compliance issues and provides reliable data that you can use to measure ROI and present to retailers.

Pro Tip: Always align coupon development with your promotions calendar. Launching coupons without planning where and when they'll hit the market can waste money and confuse both shoppers and retail partners.

Advertising

Promotion through paid media is often the most visible expression of a brand, yet many young companies misunderstand its purpose. Exposure alone is not the objective. Effective investment should support the path from discovery to purchase and then to repeat behavior, always in harmony with where items are actually available. When awareness is created without access, money is wasted and shoppers are disappointed. The smartest operators therefore concentrate spending where it can influence real buying decisions and be measured against sell through.

Digital Advertising

Digital advertising has become the backbone of modern CPG communication because precision targeting and performance tracking are built in. Social platforms such as Meta, TikTok, YouTube, and Pinterest allow brands to demonstrate usage, personality, and lifestyle fit in visually compelling ways. Search programs on Google capture shoppers who are already hunting for solutions within the category. Once distribution is secured, retailer ecosystems such as Amazon, Walmart Connect, and Kroger Precision

Marketing become especially powerful because they reach consumers close to the moment of checkout. For brands with limited budgets, this proximity to purchase frequently produces the most defensible return.

Influencer Marketing

Influencer marketing succeeds because trust transfers from creator to product. Audiences often believe a familiar voice in their feed more readily than a polished commercial. Partnerships may include paid posts, recipe integrations, or longer term ambassador relationships that build continuity. The deciding factor is rarely audience size. A smaller but devoted community can generate stronger conversion than a massive but passive following.

Print Advertising

Print advertising plays a narrower but still meaningful role. Features in respected outlets can signal legitimacy and maturity, particularly to retail buyers or financial partners. Trade media such as Progressive Grocer or Supermarket News, along with consumer titles like Bon Appétit and EatingWell, often function more as reputation builders than direct sales engines.

Out of Home Advertising (OOH)

Out of home advertising delivers scale and unavoidable visibility through billboards, transit placements, and high traffic digital screens. It can legitimize a brand overnight in a local market, but only when shoppers can immediately find the item nearby. Without distribution density, the impression fades into frustration rather than conversion.

In-Store Advertising

In-store advertising reaches consumers at the decisive instant. Shelf communication, aisle signage, audio, circulars, and sampling interrupt routine and can redirect the basket in seconds. When these efforts coincide with price incentives, the lift can be dramatic because awareness and value appear simultaneously.

Emerging Channels

Beyond traditional options, emerging channels continue to reshape the landscape. Audio partnerships, streaming placements, and hyperlocal mobile targeting offer fresh ways to surround defined audiences. Platforms like Hulu illustrate how television style storytelling can now be bought with far more flexibility. Still, experimentation should begin modestly. Novelty alone does not guarantee effectiveness, and disciplined testing protects precious capital.

In the end, advertising performs best when it behaves like a guide rather than a megaphone, leading interested consumers smoothly from inspiration to the shelf where your product is waiting.

Key Takeaway

For CPG startups, advertising works best when it's targeted, trackable, and tied directly to retail or e-commerce availability. Avoid spraying dollars across flashy platforms, focus on mediums where you can see a direct connection between ad spend and product movement.

Pro Tip: Every advertising dollar should answer two questions:

1. *Am I building awareness among the right consumers?*

2. *Can I measure whether this effort moved product?*

Guerrilla Marketing

Guerrilla activity is about creating disproportionate attention through imagination, speed, and closeness to real shoppers rather than deep pockets. For emerging food and beverage CPG companies, it is often the earliest way to generate trial, conversation, and retail excitement before larger media budgets are realistic. When executed properly, these moments feel unexpected but perfectly placed, and they point clearly to where someone can purchase immediately. When executed poorly, they feel intrusive, careless, or worse, noncompliant. Success lives at the intersection of creativity, authorization, and measurable outcomes.

At the heart of strong execution is timing and environment. Dense foot traffic where appetite, routine, and convenience meet, commuter corridors, beaches, campuses, office clusters, can produce more impact in ninety minutes than weeks of passive advertising. A single clear promise will outperform a crowded message every time. Sampling must flow seamlessly toward purchase, typically through a quick scan that leads to a store finder or product page, ideally paired with a limited incentive. Even the most scrappy set up should still appear professional, organized, and respectful of the space. And every event should be built to capture learning, conversations, scans, offers redeemed, and the effect on nearby sell through in the weeks that follow.

Certain field tactics repeatedly prove effective. Rapid sampling bursts move large numbers of tastes in concentrated windows. Retail adjacent intercepts bridge curiosity and basket by guiding shoppers straight to the aisle. Workplace tastings convert captive groups and often trigger social sharing within companies. Fitness studios provide aligned audiences already primed for functional benefits. Student representatives can create a repeatable drumbeat of peer driven advocacy. Small experiential carts or pop ups deliver visual theater without the cost of major exhibitions. Community service tie ins generate goodwill while still directing participants toward purchase. Partnerships with mobile kitchens add built in crowds and content opportunities. Whatever the format, pairing physical activation with localized digital reinforcement amplifies the result far beyond the street corner.

None of this works without attention to permissions and safety. Municipal rules may require permits. Private property demands written approval. Retailers frequently maintain strict requirements around who can sample and how. Health regulations, allergen communication, and insurance certificates protect both brand and host. Accessibility, traffic flow, and cleanup matter. So does claim discipline. A concise field playbook that covers set up, scripts, escalation contacts, and contingencies can prevent small mistakes from becoming expensive ones.

Creative discipline is equally important. The most effective encounters open with a tight hook, support it with one memorable proof point, and close with a single action. Portable signage, strong retailer cues, and scannable codes remove friction. The conversation should be brief, warm, and repeatable, allowing teams to maintain energy while reaching many people.

Moments in the field must translate into numbers. Elements such as labor and product are easy to count. Interactions, scans, and redemptions begin to reveal efficiency. The real prize is what happens next, whether velocities in surrounding stores improve and whether that improvement sustains. Comparing performance before and after each activation transforms anecdote into strategy.

Finally, integration multiplies value. Teasing activity ahead of time prepares the audience. Live coverage extends reach in real time. Follow up communication converts first purchase into second. Sharing results with buyers demonstrates partnership and professionalism.

Final Word

Guerrilla marketing is all about being precisely present where your best customer already is, with a sample in one hand and a frictionless path to purchase in the other. Keep it legal, human, and measurable. If shoppers smile, retail customers nod, and your velocities climb, you're doing it right.

BONUS - Experiential Marketing

Building Fully Immersive, Out-of-Store Brand Experiences

Experiential marketing takes your brand off the shelf and into the real world. While in-store demos introduce a product, immersive experiences invite consumers to step into your brand, understand it, feel it, and remember it. For CPG founders, this is one of the most powerful ways to create emotional connection, accelerate trial, and build lasting loyalty beyond a single purchase moment.

At its best, experiential marketing is not an event for the sake of visibility. It is a deliberate extension of your brand strategy. Every element, from location to design to interaction, should reinforce your positioning and clearly communicate why your product exists. When executed well, these experiences do more than generate awareness. They create memory, and memory drives repeat behavior.

What Makes an Experience "Immersive"

An immersive experience engages more than one sense and

more than one touchpoint. It moves beyond passive sampling and creates an environment where consumers can interact with your product in a meaningful way.

This may include:

- A physical environment that reflects your brand's origin, ingredients, or lifestyle
- Guided tastings or preparation moments that showcase how the product is used
- Storytelling elements that connect consumers to your mission or sourcing
- Interactive components that invite participation rather than observation

For example, a beverage brand might create a pop-up lounge that reflects the mood and ingredients of the product, while a snack brand might design a tasting experience that highlights sourcing, texture, and pairing. The goal is not scale, it is depth.

Strategic Objectives of Experiential Marketing

Experiential marketing should always serve a clear purpose. Common objectives include:

- Driving high-quality product trial in a controlled environment
- Building brand awareness among a targeted audience
- Creating content for digital and social amplification
- Strengthening relationships with retailers, buyers, and partners
- Reinforcing premium positioning or brand differentiation

Unlike traditional marketing, where impressions are the primary metric, experiential focuses on engagement and conversion quality.

Designing for Impact

Effective experiences are intentional and tightly aligned with your brand. A few guiding principles:

Clarity of Concept

Consumers should understand your brand within moments of entering the space. The experience should feel cohesive, not fragmented.

Product Integration

Your product should be central, not secondary. The experience exists to elevate the product, not distract from it.

Audience Alignment

Choose locations and formats that match your target consumer. A well-executed small event with the right audience is far more valuable than a large, unfocused activation.

Operational Simplicity

Experiences should be designed with execution in mind. Overly complex setups can lead to operational strain and inconsistent delivery.

Measuring Success

Experiential marketing is often viewed as difficult to measure, but strong programs include clear metrics from the start. These may include:

- Samples distributed and trial-to-purchase conversion
- Email or SMS sign-ups
- Social engagement and content reach
- Retail lift in surrounding stores
- Follow-on orders from participating retailers or partners

Tracking mechanisms, such as QR codes, digital sign-ups, or localized sales analysis, help connect the experience back to measurable outcomes.

Budget Considerations
Experiential marketing can range from lean to highly produced.
Key cost areas include:

- Venue or space rental
- Event design and build-out
- Staffing and brand ambassadors
- Product sampling and preparation
- Permits, insurance, and logistics
- Content capture (photo and video)

Founders should approach experiential as a strategic investment. A single well-executed experience can deliver more impact than multiple fragmented efforts.

Where Experiential Fits in Your Growth Strategy
Experiential marketing is most effective when it complements your broader go-to-market plan. It can be used to:

- Support a retail launch in a specific market
- Introduce a new product or line extension
- Strengthen brand presence in a key region
- Generate buzz ahead of broader distribution

It is not a replacement for trade marketing or retail execution, but a powerful layer that enhances both.

Experiential marketing allows your brand to exist beyond packaging and placement. It gives consumers a reason to connect, remember, and share. For founders, it is an opportunity to bring the brand to life in a way that no shelf ever could.

Cause Marketing

Cause marketing reaches beyond transactions and connects a company to a social, environmental, or community priority in a way that is meaningful and credible. Modern shoppers, particularly younger cohorts, increasingly expect the brands in their baskets to contribute to something larger than profit. For founders, this expectation presents an opportunity. When the commitment is genuine, it can deepen loyalty, strengthen reputation, and generate measurable benefit for communities connected to the business.

The value shows up in multiple directions. Consumers develop emotional attachment when they understand what a company stands for. In competitive aisles where taste and price may be similar, a visible commitment can distinguish one product from another. Retail partners often welcome suppliers whose missions reinforce their own sustainability and responsibility objectives. Internal teams feel it as well. People are more energized when their daily work contributes to outcomes they respect.

Effective initiatives share a common thread. The mission is integrated into operations rather than appearing as a short lived publicity effort. A snack producer that funds meals through every purchase, a coffee roaster that invests in forest regeneration with transparent reporting, or a beverage company redesigning packaging while supporting cleanup efforts are not simply running campaigns, they are expressing identity. Because the work is structural, the message feels believable.

Before moving forward, leaders benefit from a careful self review. The cause should fit naturally with the brand narrative and the realities of the category. Resources must extend beyond communications into actual dollars, partnerships, or operational change. Progress needs to be demonstrable so that shoppers, retailers, and financial partners can see evidence rather than aspiration. Perhaps most importantly, the commitment should remain relevant years from now, not just in the next quarter.

Food and beverage CPG companies often gravitate toward several areas of impact. Hunger relief and food access connect directly to the purpose of feeding people and therefore resonate immediately. Environmental stewardship, from packaging choices to climate initiatives, aligns with rising consumer expectations around planetary responsibility. Support for farmers and agricultural communities ties brands to the origin of ingredients and reinforces authenticity. Health and nutrition programs position companies as partners in well being. Efforts advancing equity and inclusion demonstrate leadership and open doors to broader audiences. Investments in local development build loyalty in the very neighborhoods where products are sold. For animal adjacent categories, welfare standards can be central to credibility with flexitarian and vegan shoppers.

The common denominator is sincerity. Audiences quickly sense when a company is pursuing headlines instead of impact. When the commitment is real, visible, and consistent, cause marketing becomes more than promotion. It becomes proof of character, and character is what sustains trust over time.

Pro Tip: Pick a cause that feels like a natural extension of your product and brand story. A granola bar brand tied to environmental reforestation feels authentic and connected. The tighter the alignment, the stronger the impact and the easier it is to communicate consistently.

Cultural Context and
Representation in Food Branding

Food carries history. It holds memory, migration, celebration, and survival within every bite. Any company that brings a culturally rooted product to market participates in shaping how that heritage is perceived and valued. In a global marketplace, portrayal is not a decorative choice. It is an obligation. The words on a label, the visuals on a package, and the narrative a founder shares all contribute to a broader understanding of whose traditions matter. When handled with care, branding can foster pride and connection while inviting discovery. When handled carelessly, it can flatten nuance or silence the very communities that created the cuisine.

Context matters because culinary traditions are inseparable from the people and places that formed them. Offering a culturally inspired product is therefore an act of translation. It requires honoring origins while welcoming new audiences with clarity and respect. Beyond ethics, this is also smart strategy. Shoppers increasingly gravitate toward companies that illuminate real histories, elevate overlooked contributors, and demonstrate sincerity rather than surface level diversity.

The distinction between representation and appropriation usually rests on intention, attribution, and shared benefit. Representation acknowledges sources, credits influence, and creates pathways for communities connected to that foodway to participate in the success that follows. Appropriation borrows aesthetics or flavors while detaching them from people and context. In practice, this means naming culinary lineages accurately, collaborating with producers or cultural stewards, and avoiding vague language that turns specificity into stereotype. Reciprocity transforms commerce into relationship.

Authenticity becomes a competitive advantage when it is grounded in truth rather than performance. Today's consumers quickly recognize disconnects between imagery and reality. Credibility grows when founders speak from lived experience, when partnerships bring real expertise, and when storytelling includes learning alongside selling. The brands that earn long term respect are those that treat culture as foundation, not theme.

Communication choices deserve the same rigor. Language should be precise, correctly rendered, and accompanied by explanations that inform instead of mystify. Visuals should convey dignity, avoiding caricature while celebrating vibrancy. Patterns, colors, and symbols carry histories of their own, and thoughtful research ensures alignment rather than misuse. The objective is not dilution for mass comfort, but accurate and artful presentation.

When companies approach culture with humility, curiosity, and care, branding becomes a form of stewardship. It preserves lineage, broadens understanding, and creates room at the table for more voices to be heard.

The Power of Representation
in the Food Industry

Representation isn't just about individual brands, it's about *shifting narratives*. For too long, certain cuisines have been underpriced, misunderstood, or misrepresented in grocery retail.

When emerging founders bring new cuisines to market with care and confidence, they help expand the definition of what belongs on the shelf.

Representation also fosters economic equity. When cultural communities have ownership and visibility in how their foods are produced, distributed, and marketed, they gain more than shelf space, they gain agency.

Pro Tip: Culture is a Living Ingredient

Culture evolves. Traditions adapt. Dishes travel, fuse, and transform. That's part of their beauty. The key is to approach cultural inspiration with curiosity, collaboration, and humility, understanding that food is both deeply personal and universally shared.

Your role as a founder is to carry that story responsibly, celebrating its roots while allowing it to flourish in new contexts.

Return on Investment
and Advertising Spend

Putting dollars behind promotions, media, or field programs is exciting, but enthusiasm without accountability is expensive. Every initiative should ultimately answer a simple question: did the investment create value for the business? Two measurements sit at the center of that evaluation, return on investment and return on advertising spend. One looks at total profitability, the other isolates marketing efficiency. Together they provide a practical framework for deciding what to repeat, what to refine, and what to stop.

Return on investment is the wider lens. It evaluates how much profit an activity generated after all associated costs are considered. If a brand funds a sampling program, the calculation would include not only the media or staffing expense, but also product, freight, temporary price reductions, and operational support. Imagine allocating ten thousand dollars to that effort and seeing eighteen thousand dollars in incremental profit tied to the program. After subtracting the initial outlay, the gain represents an eighty percent return. This view is powerful because it reveals whether the initiative strengthened the company financially, not simply whether it created buzz.

Return on advertising spend narrows the focus to the performance of paid media itself. Instead of incorporating every operational expense, it asks how much tracked revenue was produced relative to what was spent on ads. A five-thousand-dollar paid social flight that delivers fifteen thousand dollars in attributable sales yields a three to one outcome, three dollars back for every dollar deployed. That ratio helps marketers understand which platforms, audiences, and creative approaches deserve additional budget.

The distinction between the two metrics is essential. Advertising might appear efficient, yet once trade funding or supply chain realities are layered in, the broader initiative could still underperform. The reverse can also be true. A campaign with modest media efficiency might unlock distribution gains or long-term loyalty that make the overall investment worthwhile.

Strong operators monitor both views simultaneously. Advertising efficiency guides tactical optimization, while total return determines whether the business is truly building profitable growth. When used together, these measures turn marketing from a gamble into a disciplined system for smarter scaling.

Calculating ROI

$$ROI = \frac{(Revenue - Ad\ Spend)}{(Ad\ Spend)} \times 100$$

Figure: Calculating ROI

Calculating ROAS

ROAS = Revenue from Ad Campaign / Cost of Ad Campaign

Figure: Calculating ROAS

Pro Tip: Don't rely on "vanity metrics" like impressions or likes alone. True marketing success is measured in incremental sales, repeat purchases, and profitability.

Ask yourself: *For every dollar I spent, what did I earn back, and how can I repeat or scale what worked?*

BONUS - Store Locators

Once your product reaches retail shelves, one of the most common questions you'll hear from consumers is simple and direct: where can I find it? A store locator answers that question by guiding shoppers to the nearest place to buy your product, whether in a physical store or online. For emerging brands, a store locator is not just a convenience tool, it's a signal of legitimacy. It shows that your brand has real-world presence and retail traction, which builds confidence with both consumers and trade partners.

A store locator is a digital feature, typically embedded on your brand's website, that allows shoppers to search for nearby retailers by ZIP code, city, or GPS location. Most are powered by third-party platforms that integrate with distributor or retailer data, ensuring locations are accurate and scalable as your distribution grows. Many modern locators also include links to online retailers or direct-to-consumer options, creating a seamless "find near me or buy now" experience that meets shoppers wherever they are.

The value of a store locator starts with driving trial. Interested consumers want the shortest path from curiosity to purchase. If they can't easily find your product, they may abandon the search or choose a competitor instead. A clear, easy-to-use locator removes friction at the moment of intent. It also builds trust and credibility. Seeing your product listed at recognizable retailers reassures shoppers that your brand is established and accessible, even if your footprint is still modest.

Store locators also support your retail relationships. Retailers appreciate brands that actively send shoppers to their stores. By highlighting their locations on your website, you reinforce the idea that you're a partner invested in driving foot traffic, not just a supplier. Over time, this can strengthen buyer relationships and support expansion conversations. In addition, many store locator platforms provide valuable data, such as search volume by geography, which can reveal where consumer interest is highest and where additional distribution may be warranted.

To be effective, a store locator must be well maintained. Keeping listings up to date is essential, outdated or inaccurate information frustrates shoppers and can damage trust. When possible, showing which SKUs are available at each location adds clarity and reduces disappointment. Including buy-online links gives shoppers an immediate alternative if a nearby store doesn't carry their preferred item. Finally, mobile optimization is critical. Most shoppers search for products on their phones, often while already on the go, so your locator should be fast, intuitive, and mobile-friendly. Done well, a store locator becomes a quiet but powerful bridge between marketing interest and retail sales.

Pro Tip: You don't need thousands of doors to justify a store locator. Even if you're in 10–20 independent stores, adding them to your website helps consumers find you and signals retail momentum.

Tools to Explore

- **Destini** – One of the most popular tools for emerging brands; integrates with distributor data like UNFI and KeHE.

- **SOCI** – Offers customizable locators with analytics.

- **Mapbox / Google Maps API** – DIY options for tech-savvy brands.

- **Distributor Partner Locators** – Some distributors provide store lists you can embed or link to.

Pro Tip: Pair your store locator with a call-to-action: *"Can't find us near you? Request us at your local store!"* This turns your locator into both a sales driver and a grassroots distribution tool.

Our Founders' Journey

Elena - Harbor Harvest Foods
(Spiced Mango Preserves)

With *Harbor Harvest Foods* now on local shelves, Elena realized that products don't sell themselves, people do. She signed up for her first in-store demo, nervously setting up her table with tiny sample spoons and a handwritten sign. By the end of the day, she'd sold nearly every jar and gained invaluable insight into what customers loved most: her story. That day, she stopped seeing demos as tasks and started seeing them as conversations, opportunities to build connection one taste at a time.

Marcus - Summit Sips (Clean
Labeled Sparkling Iced Tea)

Marcus launched his first digital ad campaign for *Summit Sips*, targeting wellness consumers through paid social and e-commerce ads. The creative was sleek, but the results were underwhelming. After diving into analytics, he realized his message sounded corporate, not human. He shifted the tone to storytelling, showing the founders' morning routines and featuring user testimonials. Engagement doubled within weeks. Marcus learned that authenticity wasn't a buzzword; it was a strategy.

Danielle - Bountiful Bites (Upcycled Snacks)

Danielle threw herself into promotion, sponsoring community runs, posting daily, and giving away free product at every opportunity. Yet her sales barely moved. A mentor helped her see the gap: she had awareness, but no *conversion strategy*. Her promotions weren't leading consumers back to stores or online carts. She regrouped, creating limited-time offers tied to specific retailers. For the first time, her visibility started translating into velocity.

Andre - Kindred Grains
(Ancient Grain Snacks)

Andre treated consumer promotion like a science. Every demo, ad, and giveaway had a purpose and a budget. He tracked *ROAS (Return on Ad Spend)* and compared demo sales to non-demo weeks. His results were modest but clear: every strategic investment paid off when aligned with store-level support. It reinforced what he already knew, in food, marketing isn't about shouting the loudest; it's about knowing when, where, and why to speak.

CHAPTER SIX

Performance Measurement and Progress

Early in my career, I learned a simple truth: what gets measured, gets managed, and what doesn't, gets missed.

I've sat in quarterly business reviews where founders couldn't explain why sales were up one month and down the next. They were working hard, spending money, and moving product, but without a system for tracking performance, they were running blind. Numbers are as much about accountability as they are about clarity. They tell you what's actually happening versus what you *think* is happening.

This chapter is about helping you see your business clearly. You'll learn how to measure sales velocity, track profitability, analyze marketing results, and evaluate the strength of your retail relationships. We'll also cover how to build systems for continuous improvement, because growth isn't always about doing more; sometimes it's about doing smarter.

As someone who has led both multi-million dollar brands and small startup teams, I can tell you this: every company, regardless of size, benefits from discipline and reflection. Progress is built on performance, and performance is built on data, insight, and action.

Velocities / Turns (Sales Metrics)

Velocity, sometimes referred to as "turns," is one of the most important retail performance metrics and one that many founders discover early on. While getting authorized at a retailer can feel like the win, velocity is what determines whether you stay. Retailers are in the business of maximizing sales per inch of shelf space, and velocity is the clearest signal of whether your product is earning its spot. A brand can secure placement once, but without movement, it will be discontinued quickly, regardless of how good the product or story may be.

Velocity measures the rate at which your product sells once it is on shelf, most commonly expressed as units sold per store per week (often abbreviated as UPSPW). This metric cuts through distribution size and focuses purely on sell-through. Rather than asking how many stores you're in, velocity answers a more important question: when shoppers see your product, do they buy it? Strong velocity indicates consumer pull, effective pricing, and clear on-shelf communication, while weak velocity signals that something is off, whether it's awareness, placement, price, or relevance.

Buyers rely heavily on velocity to make decisions. They benchmark your performance against the category average and against direct competitors on the same shelf. If your item consistently underperforms, it becomes a candidate for removal during the next reset. On the other hand, strong velocity makes your product more attractive for promotions, displays, and expanded distribution. Retailers are far more willing to invest in endcaps, features, or additional facings when the data shows your product moves efficiently. In many cases, distributors and larger retailers will not approve expansion into new regions or stores without proof that your product can hit minimum velocity thresholds in existing doors.

The term "turns" is often used interchangeably with velocity, but it emphasizes the inventory side of the equation. Turns refer to how often product sells through and is replenished over a given period. From a retailer's perspective, high turns mean inventory dollars are being used efficiently and shelf space is generating strong returns. Products with low turns tie up cash, increase the risk of shrink or expiration, and ultimately hurt category performance. For founders, understanding both velocity and turns helps align your goals with the retailer's priorities. The objective isn't just to get on shelf, it's to move consistently, earn repeat space, and prove that your brand is a reliable contributor to the category's growth.

How to Measure Velocity

$$\text{Velocity} = \frac{\text{Total Units Sold}}{\text{Number of Stores X Number of Weeks}}$$

Formula: Calculating Velocity

Example:

- You sold 2,000 units in 10 stores over 4 weeks.
- Velocity = 2,000 ÷ (10 × 4) = 50 units/store/week.

What Buyers Expect

- Category norms vary. In salty snacks, strong velocity may be 10–20 UPSPW; in refrigerated beverages, 30–50 UPSPW.

- Some buyers require you to hit specific thresholds (ex., *"We expect at least 15 units per store per week in this category"*).

- Premium or niche products may get a little more leeway, but they still must perform.

Founder Tips

- **Track Early:** Even small accounts (farmers markets, independents) give you velocity data. Document it and bring it to buyer meetings.

- **Compare to Category:** Don't just share your number, show how it stacks up against category averages.

- **Promotions Boost, But Sustained Sales Matter:** Promotions can spike velocity, but buyers look for repeat turns after the deal ends.

- **Distributor Feedback:** Distributors monitor turns too. Low velocity products tie up warehouse space and risk being dropped.

Pro Tip: Never pitch a buyer with only total sales. Always show velocity, it's the cleanest metric of consumer demand. Strong velocity is your ticket to expansion.

Key Performance Indicators (KPIs) for Food and Beverage Founders

When you're building a food brand, passion, creativity, and a great plan are the blueprint, but metrics are your compass. Key Performance Indicators, or KPIs, are the measurable data points that tell you how your business is performing, where you're excelling, and where you need to refine your strategy.

While early-stage founders often focus on surface-level results, sales totals, followers, or press mentions, industry leaders know that sustainable success comes from tracking the right *combination* of indicators. These metrics reveal not only what's happening, but *why*.

Why KPIs Matter

KPIs keep you grounded in reality. They transform intuition into evidence and help you:

- Evaluate progress toward your business goals.
- Make informed decisions about pricing, promotions, and production.
- Spot early warning signs before they become major problems.

- Communicate impact clearly to investors, partners, and retailers.

Data doesn't replace instinct, it refines it.

Categories of KPIs

Growth becomes manageable the moment performance is translated into numbers that can be monitored, compared, and improved. In food and beverage CPG, the most effective scorecards typically fall into five clusters: sales and distribution, financial health, marketing and engagement, operational efficiency, and consumer behavior. Looking at only one creates blind spots. Studying them together reveals whether demand is real, profitable, and repeatable.

Sales and Distribution Metrics

These indicators show how product is moving where it is available and whether expansion is happening in the right doors. Buyers and distributors live in this data, so founders must be fluent in it. Velocity, commonly expressed as units per store per week, tells the trade how quickly items sell relative to the shelf space they occupy. Sell through measures how much of what was shipped actually made it into shoppers' baskets, offering a reality check on demand planning and helping prevent excess inventory. Coverage metrics such as ACV and weighted distribution reveal the quality of distribution, clarifying whether a brand is present in stores that truly matter to the category.

Momentum is captured through sales growth, tracked across months, quarters, or years to show trajectory. Meanwhile, out of stocks expose operational friction. Even strong demand cannot translate into revenue if the shelf is empty, so persistent gaps often signal forecasting or replenishment issues that need immediate correction.

Financial Health Metrics

Top line growth is exciting, but durability comes from profitable growth. Gross margin shows what remains after direct production costs, giving insight into pricing power and manufacturing discipline. Operating margin widens the aperture by including payroll, marketing, and overhead, revealing whether the enterprise structure is sustainable.

EBITDA is frequently used in investor conversations because it normalizes performance across companies and strips out capital structure differences. Liquidity is reflected in the cash conversion cycle, which measures how quickly investments in inventory return as cash. The shorter the cycle, the more flexible the company becomes. Unit and case costs round out the picture, grounding strategy in SKU level reality and informing everything from promotions to channel mix.

Marketing and Engagement Metrics

Attention is only useful if it leads to action. Customer acquisition cost clarifies how expensive it is to bring in each new buyer, while customer lifetime value estimates the total revenue that relationship will generate. Healthy businesses typically see lifetime value far outpace acquisition expense.

Repeat purchase rate is one of the clearest signals of product market fit. If consumers come back, the promise delivered. Digital visibility measures such as impressions and engagement reveal whether messaging resonates or simply passes by unnoticed. Redemption rates on coupons or offers add another layer, demonstrating how effectively incentives convert curiosity into purchase.

Operational Efficiency Metrics

Behind every great brand sits a machine that must run smoothly. Order fulfillment rates confirm whether customers receive what they requested on time and in full. Inventory turnover indicates how quickly product cycles through the system, highlighting risks of spoilage or tied up capital.

Shrink and waste quietly erode margins when left unmanaged. Monitoring them keeps profitability intact. Production yield helps evaluate manufacturing performance, especially when working with co packers, by comparing expected output with actual results. Freight cost per case influences landed margin and, ultimately, pricing strategy in each channel.

Consumer Metrics

As distribution expands, the central question becomes how deeply the brand is embedding itself into households. Penetration measures how many homes have purchased at least once, providing a sense of reach. Frequency then shows whether those homes are returning often enough to create habit.

Share of wallet illustrates competitive strength, revealing how much of category spend flows to the brand versus alternatives. Awareness and perception, though sometimes softer, are equally vital. Surveys and sentiment analysis uncover whether consumers recognize the brand, trust it, and associate it with the intended attributes.

How to Track KPIs Effectively

- Start Small, Scale Smart: Focus on the handful of KPIs most relevant to your business stage.

- Automate When Possible: Use dashboards (Shopify Analytics, QuickBooks, Google Data Studio, SPINS, or NielsenIQ) to track and visualize performance.

- Review Monthly or Quarterly: Regular rhythm builds awareness and accountability.

- Benchmark Against the Industry: Compare your results to category standards to understand whether your numbers are good or just good-looking.

- Act on the Insights: Data is only valuable if it leads to a decision, adjustment, or improvement.

Pro Tip: Balance Growth with Efficiency

A brand that grows distribution faster than its velocity, or acquires customers faster than it can fulfill orders, isn't truly scaling. KPIs help you spot these imbalances early and redirect your energy toward *profitable, sustainable* growth.

Syndicated Data

At a certain point in your growth journey, buyers and investors will start asking questions like, *"What is your ACV?"* In the world of consumer packaged goods, syndicated data is essentially the industry's scoreboard. It's how retailers, analysts, and competitors objectively measure performance across sales, distribution, share, pricing, and growth. While it can be expensive, syndicated data becomes increasingly important once you're aiming to scale beyond regional success and compete head-to-head with established brands.

Syndicated data refers to sales and market information collected from retailers and distributors, aggregated by third-party data firms, and sold through subscription-based services. Unlike your internal sales reports, which only reflect what you ship or invoice, syndicated data shows what actually sells through at retail and how your performance compares to the rest of the category. It typically covers dollar and unit sales, distribution metrics such as all-commodity volume (ACV), pricing trends, and promotional effectiveness, providing a more complete and unbiased view of your business.

This data matters because it lends credibility with retailers. Buyers rely on syndicated data to validate brand performance at scale, and many are reluctant to expand distribution without it. It also allows for true competitive benchmarking, helping you understand whether you're gaining or losing share, how fast competitors are growing, and where your pricing or promotions may be over or underperforming. From a strategic standpoint, syndicated data informs smarter decisions around pricing, promotional depth, assortment, and geographic expansion. For investors, it's a familiar and trusted language. Being able to reference third-party data instead of anecdotal wins strengthens your fundraising narrative and signals operational maturity.

Several providers dominate the syndicated data landscape. NielsenIQ offers the broadest coverage across grocery, mass, drug, and club channels, making it especially valuable for brands expanding into conventional and mass retail. Its reports are commonly used to track ACV, distribution gains, pricing, and promotional lift. Circana, which includes the legacy IRI and NPD business, is particularly strong in grocery, drug, and convenience channels and is known for deep shopper insights, forecasting tools, and detailed promotional analytics. SPINS is the go-to source for natural, organic, specialty, and wellness categories. Its attribute-level tracking, such as gluten-free, plant-based, or keto, is especially helpful for emerging better-for-you brands looking to position themselves within fast-growing subsegments.

For founders, the key is timing. Syndicated data subscriptions can cost anywhere from $30,000 to well over $100,000 annually, so it rarely makes sense to invest too early. Many brokers and distributors can provide limited data cuts as part of their service, which can be enough to support buyer conversations in the early stages. It's also smart to leverage retailer-provided data first. Large retailers like Kroger and Walmart offer internal data portals that give visibility into sales, pricing, and promotions within their own systems, often at little or no additional cost.

Pro Tip: When you do invest, make sure you have someone on your team (or a consultant) who can interpret the data. Numbers are only as valuable as the insights you extract from them.

BONUS - COMPARING SYNDICATED DATA PLATFORMS

Founders often ask: "Which syndicated data provider should I use?" The truth is, each has strengths and weaknesses depending on your category, growth stage, and retail channel. Below is a side-by-side comparison to help you evaluate which is right for your business.

NielsenIQ (Nielsen)

Channel Coverage: Grocery, Mass, Drug, Club, Dollar, and many specialty retailers.

Strengths:

- The gold standard for mainstream CPG categories.

- Deep insights into pricing, promotions, and distribution (ACV).

- Widely recognized by retailers and investors.

Limitations:

- Very expensive for smaller brands ($50,000+/yr).

- Less granular in natural/specialty product attributes.

Best For: Mid-stage to scaling brands expanding into mass grocery and big-box retail.

Circana (Formerly IRI)

Channel Coverage: Grocery, Mass, Drug, Convenience, Dollar, and Club.

Strengths:

- Strong in multi-channel coverage.

- Known for advanced shopper insights, forecasting, and panel data.

- Provides robust promotional lift analysis.

Limitations:

- Similar cost to Nielsen (high investment).

- Less specialized in natural/specialty attributes.

Best For: Brands ready for national scale who want a broad view across channels.

SPINS

Channel Coverage: Natural, Specialty, Organic, Health and Wellness, Independent Natural Chains.

Strengths:

- Attribute-level tracking (ex., gluten-free, plant-based, keto).

- Best for emerging brands in natural, organic, or wellness.

- Costs are more accessible than Nielsen/Circana (though still significant: $20,000+/yr).

Limitations:

- Coverage is weaker in mass and conventional grocery.

- Retailers outside of natural may not rely on SPINS as heavily.

Best For: Early to mid-stage brands targeting natural/specialty channels or wellness-driven growth stories.

Pro Tips:

- If you're in the natural space, start with SPINS.
- If you're scaling into mainstream grocery, NielsenIQ or Circana will carry more weight with buyers.
- If you're still early, lean on retailer portals, distributors, or brokers for syndicated data snapshots before signing a big contract.

Reading and Understanding Syndicated Data

Access to platforms such as Nielsen, SPINS, or Circana can feel like being handed the keys to the kingdom, yet the true advantage comes from interpretation. Buyers are not searching for dense printouts. They want clarity, direction, and confidence. The task is to translate numbers into a persuasive explanation of why a brand will strengthen their assortment, attract shoppers, and contribute incremental dollars.

A strong presentation begins by zooming out to the category itself. Demonstrate whether it is rising, softening, or holding steady, and anchor the conversation in recognizable metrics such as total dollars and year over year change. This establishes context and signals that you understand the retailer's business, not just your own ambitions. When a buyer hears that a multibillion dollar segment continues to grow at a healthy rate, the door opens to a conversation about innovation and expansion rather than replacement.

From there, move closer to where energy is building. Subsegments and product attributes often reveal the real engines of growth. Perhaps lower sugar options are accelerating, plant based claims are gaining share, or premium formats are pulling shoppers upward. When your positioning lives inside one of these faster moving pockets, the connection becomes obvious. You are no longer pitching an item, you are presenting a solution aligned with where consumers are already heading.

Only after the landscape is clear should the spotlight turn to your own performance. Velocity becomes the headline. If units move quickly where distribution already exists, you have evidence of demand. Pair that with growth rates that exceed the broader market and you create reassurance. The message is simple, shoppers are voting with their wallets.

Next, convert proof into value for that specific retailer. Every merchant is chasing incrementality, stronger margins, and new consumer segments. Show how your brand ladders into those priorities. Model potential dollar contribution. Clarify how your shopper differs from or expands the current base. When done well, the buyer can easily picture success on their shelves.

Presentation matters as much as substance. A few clean visuals will outperform dozens of crowded tables. Trend lines make momentum intuitive. Side by side comparisons dramatize outperformance. Restraint communicates mastery.

Finally, credibility grows when the story holds up across time-frames. Long views reveal structural change while shorter windows highlight present acceleration. Consistency between them tells a buyer that the opportunity is real and durable, not a temporary spike.

When insight, relevance, and proof come together, data stops being abstract. It becomes a narrative the retailer can confidently retell internally, and that is what ultimately earns placement.

Putting It Together: A Simple Data Story Arc

- The Category Is Growing: Prove consumers want the category.
- A Sub-Segment Is Winning: Show where the action is happening.
- Our Brand Outperforms: Demonstrate why you're better positioned.
- Your Retailer Wins by Adding Us: Translates to incremental sales.

. . .

Pro Tip: Syndicated data isn't just for buyer meetings. Use it internally to prioritize channels, optimize pricing, and shape marketing. The same insights that persuade retailers should guide your strategic decisions.

Planning Ahead: Understanding
ACV (All Commodity Volume)

Highlighted in the previous section, ACV is a metric that you'll start hearing buyers, brokers, and investors reference as your brand grows. ACV is one of the most important distribution metrics in retail because it measures *how much of the market you're actually reaching*, not just how many stores carry your product. Understanding ACV helps you set realistic sales expectations, evaluate distribution wins more accurately, and tell a clearer growth story as your brand scales.

At its core, ACV represents the total sales volume of all products sold in a given market or channel, expressed as a percentage. Put simply, ACV tells you how much of the market's "weight" you're covering. If your product is sold in retailers that collectively account for 30 percent of total grocery sales in the U.S., then your ACV coverage is 30 percent. This makes ACV fundamentally different from store count. One hundred small independent stores do not carry the same market weight as one hundred high-volume national stores like Walmart.

This distinction is exactly why ACV matters so much. It reflects the *quality* of your distribution, not just the quantity. A brand with limited doors but strong ACV may have far more growth momentum than a brand with many doors but low market coverage. Buyers and investors rely on ACV as a benchmark for growth because it shows how much runway you still have. If your competitors are distributed across 70 percent ACV and you're only at 15 percent, that gap helps explain differences in scale and also highlights future opportunity.

To make this more concrete, imagine the U.S. natural grocery channel represents $10 billion in annual sales. If your brand is distributed in retailers that collectively generate $2 billion of that volume, your ACV coverage is 20 percent. That means you're reaching one-fifth of the channel's total sales base. Even if your velocities are strong, your total sales will naturally be capped until ACV expands. This is why ACV is often discussed alongside velocity. Velocity tells you how well you sell *where you are*, while ACV tells you how big your potential can be as distribution widens.

For founders, the biggest trap is confusing ACV with door count. It's tempting to celebrate being in hundreds of stores, but if those stores represent a small slice of category sales, your growth ceiling remains limited. A handful of regional or national chains can sometimes deliver more ACV than years of incremental independent wins. That doesn't make independents unimportant, they're often critical for proof of concept, learning, and early velocity, but ACV helps you see where scale will ultimately come from.

Planning ahead with ACV allows you to be more disciplined and credible in your forecasting. Many emerging brands track ACV growth in stages, for example moving from 5 percent to 20 percent, then 50 percent over time. If your revenue projections assume 50 percent ACV coverage but your current distribution only represents 10 percent, your forecasts will almost certainly miss the mark. Conversely, clearly showing how you plan to expand ACV over time helps buyers and investors understand your growth path in a grounded, data-driven way.

The good news is that you don't have to calculate ACV entirely on your own. Syndicated data providers like NielsenIQ, Circana (formerly IRI), and SPINS track ACV across channels and categories. If you don't yet have direct access to these services, your broker, distributor, or retail partners can often provide estimates. Used thoughtfully, ACV becomes one of your most powerful planning tools, helping you align ambition with reality and growth with strategy.

SKU Rationalization

Letting go of products can feel like defeat. Every flavor, format, and extension carries effort, optimism, and identity. Yet retail operates on productivity, not sentiment. Space is finite, buyers track movement relentlessly, and slow items can weaken negotiations for the rest of the line. Rationalizing the assortment is therefore not retreat, it is leadership.

At its heart, SKU rationalization is a disciplined review of what deserves to remain, what should be retired, and where additional focus can unlock growth. The objective is to build a lineup in which each item contributes meaningfully to revenue, margin, and brand clarity. When a portfolio is tight and purposeful, retailers see a partner who understands how to help the shelf perform rather than crowd it.

This discipline strengthens trust. Merchants prefer suppliers who can evaluate reality and make adjustments before being asked. Demonstrating a willingness to prune signals maturity and makes future innovation conversations easier. It shows that decisions will be grounded in performance, not emotion.

The financial implications are just as important. Every item carries hidden weight, forecasting, packaging inventories, minimum production runs, warehousing, trade funding, and administrative complexity. When weaker performers linger, resources that could fuel winners become diluted. A narrower mix often improves working capital and frees marketing dollars for the products most likely to scale.

Operationally, simplification creates momentum. Longer production runs, cleaner logistics, fewer pick errors, and stronger fill rates make life easier for partners across the chain. Distributors and co-packers value predictability, and retailers reward brands that are easy to execute.

Shoppers feel the difference too. Excess variety can create hesitation. A focused set makes the decision easier, reinforces what the brand stands for, and highlights the heroes.

Another critical lens is cannibalization. When too many similar items sit side by side, they often steal sales from each other rather than attracting new buyers. The brand may appear busy, but total volume remains flat while complexity rises. By trimming overlapping products and concentrating demand behind clear winners, you strengthen velocities, reduce confusion, and present a more powerful block on shelf. Retailers would rather see fewer items that turn fast than many that compete internally for the same purchase.

The evaluation itself should be rigorous. Start with velocity, because movement determines survival. Compare each item to internal peers and to the broader set. Layer in profitability, since volume without margin may not justify continuation. Look at repeat behavior to understand whether purchases represent loyalty or curiosity. Listen carefully to merchants, they often see trouble before reports do. Examine whether an item truly adds incremental sales or merely divides attention away from top performers. And remember that a product might still earn its place if it plays a specific strategic role, serving a key account, anchoring a price tier, or creating seasonal excitement.

When founders approach rationalization with objectivity, the result is not a smaller business. It is a sharper one, better positioned to win space, earn trust, and grow with intention.

The Process

1. **Collect Data:** Review syndicated data, retailer scorecards, and internal sales.

2. **Rank SKUs:** Stack rank from strongest to weakest on sales, margin, and velocities.

3. **Identify Underperformers:** Flag those consistently below threshold benchmarks.

4. **Assess Role:** Decide if weak SKUs have strategic value or should be discontinued.

5. **Act Decisively:** Sunset SKUs quickly and communicate with partners.

Real-World Example

A snack brand launched with six flavors. After two years, the data showed:

- Two flavors drove 70% of sales.
- Two flavors lagged far below velocity benchmarks.
- One seasonal SKU performed strongly but only for 3 months.

The founder rationalized down to the two core flavors + one seasonal. The result:

- Lower production costs.
- Higher average velocities across the board.
- Easier retail conversations with a focused, proven lineup.

SKU rationalization doesn't mean failure, it means focus. Stronger, more disciplined assortments are easier to grow and scale. Remember, it's better to be known for three SKUs that fly off the shelf than for eight SKUs that limp along.

Pro Tip: Do your own rationalization before the retailer does it for you. If you wait until a buyer decides to cut your weak SKUs, you lose control of the narrative.

Innovation

Innovation keeps a packaged food and beverage brand alive in the eyes of shoppers and relevant in the minds of buyers. It signals energy, ambition, and partnership. At the same time, novelty for its own sake can become expensive theater. Without discipline, new items multiply complexity, blur positioning, and scatter resources that should be strengthening proven performers. The most successful companies treat innovation as a strategic lever, not a creative impulse.

The reason it matters is simple. Consumers are naturally drawn to what feels new, whether that is a seasonal twist, a different format, or an added benefit that matches evolving lifestyles. Retailers are equally motivated. Freshness in the assortment gives them reasons to reset shelves, create displays, and tell shoppers there is something worth discovering. Brands that anticipate where demand is moving often secure disproportionate attention, because they arrive with solutions before the rest of the aisle catches up. When done well, innovation becomes a visible expression of relevance.

What separates smart launches from costly experiments is insight. Every addition should be anchored in evidence, category growth patterns, attribute expansion, unmet needs, shopper migration, or emerging occasions. If low sugar is gaining share faster than the total set, that is a signal. If multipacks are accelerating in club while single serves stall, that is direction. If younger households are entering through global flavors or functional benefits, that is opportunity. Innovation built on these shifts gives buyers confidence because it aligns with where their business is headed, not just where your imagination wandered.

Newness can take many shapes. Sometimes it is a simple line extension that broadens flavor appeal or creates a seasonal moment. Sometimes it is format, moving from pantry to refrigerated, from individual to family size, or from bottle to stick pack for portability. Functional upgrades may answer rising interest in protein, gut health, or energy support. Packaging improvements can deliver convenience or environmental progress. At other times, the smartest move is channel specific, tailoring pack architecture to the economics and missions of club, convenience, or foodservice. Each pathway is valid when it ladders back to strategy.

Behind every success is a structured path from idea to shelf. Inspiration should flow from real inputs, consumer feedback, retailer conversations, competitive white space, and credible trend data. From there comes filtering, where feasibility, margin structure, and brand alignment are tested honestly. Small runs and prototypes expose issues early. Limited releases or regional placements generate proof without excessive risk. Only after performance validates demand should broader commercialization follow. This rhythm allows creativity while protecting the business.

The hazards are real and should be faced directly. More items mean more ingredients, more packaging components, more forecasts, and more chances for error. They require marketing oxygen and trade investment. They can exhaust buyers who prefer predictability. And, most importantly, they can cannibalize, shifting purchases from one of your SKUs to another without expanding total volume. In that scenario, effort rises while results stand still.

Guardrails prevent that outcome. The first is authenticity. Trends are powerful, but chasing every one erodes identity. The second is validation. Early data, even from a small footprint, is more persuasive than optimism. The third is support. Products rarely succeed quietly, they need storytelling, placement, and activation. The fourth is portfolio balance. Innovation should strengthen the core, attract new users, open new occasions, or raise price realization, not distract from the engines already working.

When insight leads and discipline follows, innovation becomes more than a pipeline. It becomes a growth narrative retailers can believe in, investors can model, and consumers can feel.

Common Approaches to Innovation

The most reliable growth in packaged food rarely comes from dramatic reinvention. It typically comes from repeatable, scalable innovation platforms that retailers understand and shoppers adopt quickly. Buyers appreciate them because they are lower risk, operations teams value them because they are manageable, and investors favor them because the upside can be modeled.

Here are the innovation lanes that consistently outperform:

Flavor Innovation

New tastes are the most familiar form of innovation and often the easiest for consumers to try.

Why it wins:
It refreshes the shelf, creates news, and invites trial without asking shoppers to change habits.

Common approaches:

- Seasonal or limited time offerings
- Heat or sweet heat upgrades
- Global and regional cuisines
- Mashups and collaborations

Retailer appeal:
Easy to merchandise, perfect for promotions, and helps reset conversations.

Line Extensions (Within the Same Platform)

This means expanding what already works.

Why it wins:
It leverages existing brand equity, production, and distribution while giving loyal shoppers new options.

Common approaches:

- New flavor families
- Premium tiers
- Kid focused or family variants
- Size variations

Retailer appeal:
Builds a stronger brand block and can improve category presence.

Format Innovation

Changing how the product is delivered rather than what it is.

Why it wins:
It unlocks new occasions and dayparts.

Common approaches:

- Grab and go
- Multipacks
- Portable
- Ready to eat versus cook

. . .

Retailer appeal:
Creates incremental usage and can open new departments.

Functional or Benefit-Led Innovation

Adding a clear, relevant job for the product to do.

Why it wins:
Health and performance cues recruit new shoppers and often justify premium pricing.

Common approaches:

- Protein enrichment
- Gut or immune support
- Energy or focus
- Reduced sugar or sodium

Retailer appeal:
Captures growth from shoppers trading up.

Packaging Innovation

Sometimes the wrapper moves faster than the recipe.

Why it wins:
Improves convenience, sustainability perception, and shelf impact.

Common approaches:

- Recyclable or compostable materials
- Premium finishes
- Reseable
- Clear windows

- Portion control

Retailer appeal:
Signals modernization and can support sustainability narratives.

Occasion-Based Innovation

Designed around when and how people use food.

Why it wins:
Occasions drive baskets. Baskets drive retailer enthusiasm.

Common approaches:

- Back to school
- Holiday editions
- Entertaining kits
- Travel friendly packs

Retailer appeal:
Supports event merchandising and secondary displays.

Channel-Specific Innovation

Adapting the product to the economics of where it sells.

Why it wins:
Fits the shopper mission of that environment.

Common approaches:

- Larger club sizes
- Higher margin convenience packs
- Foodservice formats
- DTC exclusives

Retailer appeal:
Shows partnership thinking.

Most successful CPG innovation is adjacent, not revolutionary. It builds from known brand equity, proven supply chains, and validated consumer behavior.

Real-World Example

A protein bar brand launched a seasonal pumpkin spice SKU for fall. It:

- Generated strong trial from new consumers.
- Reinforced the brand's positioning as on-trend and flexible.
- Drove a 15% sales lift during Q4 without hurting core SKU sales.

By keeping it seasonal and controlled, the innovation built buzz without overwhelming operations.

Pro Tip: Innovation should be a growth lever, not a distraction. The most successful startups balance steady core SKU performance with a disciplined pipeline of thoughtful, well-supported innovation.

Channel Expansion

Channel expansion becomes the next logical move once product market fit is established, yet it is not simply a matter of adding doors. Every retail environment operates with its own economics, shopper behaviors, and expectations for support. Moving too broadly or prematurely can dilute focus, strain working capital, and weaken performance in the very places that built the brand. Smart growth is about sequencing, choosing where, when, and how to enter new outlets so momentum compounds rather than fragments.

Expanding distribution opens access to new consumers and incremental revenue streams. It also reassures buyers that the brand can travel, perform, and adapt beyond its original base. A presence across multiple formats increases visibility in the market and reduces dependence on any single partner, providing insulation if one account slows, resets, or changes strategy.

Before making the leap, founders need to pressure test readiness. Current items should already be meeting or exceeding velocity expectations. The financial model must be able to absorb additional slotting, promotional commitments, and deductions. Operations must handle greater volume along with added complexity in routing, forecasting, and customer requirements. Equally important, the target outlet has to match how shoppers use the product. Expansion should complement existing distribution, not siphon energy from it.

Growth can take many forms. Brands frequently validate themselves in natural or specialty environments before approaching conventional grocery. Others transition from those curated shelves into mass once awareness and repeat purchase patterns are strong. Some later adapt pack sizes and value equations for club, while others broaden reach through foodservice or build direct relationships via e-commerce. Each move asks the company to level up in different ways.

The healthiest path tends to be phased. Win in a tight geographic footprint where demos, merchandising, and supply can be tightly managed. Extend to multi-unit chains within regions that remain operationally realistic. Only then pursue national placements, when the organization has the infrastructure, marketing muscle, and cash resilience to support the scale.

Moving too fast carries real consequences. Teams become overstretched, execution suffers, and retailers notice quickly. Underperformance in one prominent account can echo across the market, making future conversations harder. At the same time, upfront costs and delayed payment cycles can compress liquidity. Expansion should feel like building on strength, not chasing validation.

When approached deliberately, new channels amplify success already in motion. When rushed, they expose weaknesses. The discipline lies in knowing the difference.

Real-World Example

A natural snack brand launched in Whole Foods and Sprouts, proving strong velocities in natural. After two years, they expanded to Target (mass) with a focused SKU set and strong promotional plan. They waited until year four to approach Costco, when their supply chain and finances could support club channel demands.

The result: steady, sustainable growth without overreaching.

. . .

Pro Tip: Channel expansion is a marathon, not a sprint. Focus on proving success in one channel before leaping to the next. When you expand strategically, each win builds momentum for the next opportunity.

BONUS - BUILDING A STRONG BUYER RELATIONSHIP

Securing placement is only the opening chapter. What determines longevity is the quality of the partnership with the person managing the category. Buyers hold the levers that affect survival, resets, assortment, facings, features, and expansion. When trust is present, opportunities surface more easily. When it is absent, even a good product can struggle. The brands that last understand they are not merely selling items, they are collaborating on growth.

A productive relationship brings tangible advantages. It stabilizes your presence when assortments are reviewed, opens doors to incremental displays or new items, and shapes how the retailer perceives you, either as a contributor to category performance or as background noise. It also matters when things go wrong. Forecast misses, service hiccups, and deductions are realities of doing business, and credibility built in advance often determines how much patience you receive.

Trust is earned. Reliability is foundational, arrive prepared, respond quickly, and follow through exactly as promised. Fluency in the numbers is equally critical. Buyers live in data, so come ready with velocities, promotional results, and clear next steps. Transparency strengthens confidence; early communication paired with a recovery plan is far better than silence. The most valued partners contribute insight, offering perspective on shoppers, trends, and whitespace, not simply another request for distribution. And always remember that time is scarce. Organized, concise conversations signal professionalism.

Relationships deepen through consistent, practical habits. Schedule regular touchpoints to review performance, not just when something is needed. Learn what success means inside their organization, then show how your initiatives support those metrics. Provide exclusives or first looks that help them shine internally. When progress happens, share the credit generously. Acknowledging partnership builds goodwill that compounds over years.

There are also predictable traps. Inflated promises undermine confidence faster than any competitor. Ignoring feedback suggests you are not listening to the customer they represent. Walking into meetings without data communicates unpreparedness. Repeated pressure for more space or activity, without proof of return, can exhaust patience. Strong partnerships are built on mutual benefit, respect, and results.

In the end, buyers champion the brands that make their jobs easier and their categories stronger. Become that partner, and doors tend to open.

Think of your buyer as a strategic partner, not just a customer. Their success is tied to your success. The stronger the partnership, the more likely they are to advocate for your brand when decisions are made behind closed doors.

Pro Tip: Buyers are people first. Small gestures, thank-you notes, timely communication, and recognizing their challenges go a long way. In an industry built on relationships, being the brand that's easy to work with is often your biggest competitive advantage.

Planning Ahead: Business Intelligence Tools (Tracking by SKU and Customer)

As your brand grows, sales data quickly becomes more complex. What once lived comfortably in a spreadsheet can turn into a confusing mix of SKUs, customers, promotions, deductions, and timing differences across accounts. Business Intelligence, or BI, tools exist to solve this exact problem. They help founders translate raw sales data into clear, actionable insights so decisions are based on facts rather than gut instinct.

BI tools are software platforms designed to collect, organize, and visualize your commercial data in one place. Instead of manually stitching together distributor reports, invoices, and retailer portals, these systems allow you to track performance by SKU, customer, region, and time period. Most present information through dashboards, charts, and automated reports that make trends easy to spot at a glance.

The real value of BI tools shows up at the SKU level. As assortments grow, it becomes critical to understand which products are driving velocity and margin and which are quietly dragging performance down. BI tools help you see patterns across retailers, identify underperforming SKUs early, and make informed decisions about discontinuations, reformulations, or line extensions before problems escalate.

They are equally powerful at the customer level. BI dashboards let you compare how different retailers or distributors are performing side by side, revealing where your brand is thriving and where it needs more attention. You can quickly identify accounts with strong velocity, those that require additional promotional support, or customers that look attractive in volume but weak in profitability once trade spend and deductions are factored in.

Another major benefit is promotional tracking. Promotions are expensive, and without clear reporting, it's easy to assume they're working simply because shipments increased. BI tools help separate true lift from volume shifting, showing whether a promotion actually improved velocity or merely pulled forward sales. This insight is essential for refining your trade spend strategy and avoiding waste.

From a planning perspective, BI tools strengthen forecasting and operational alignment. Historical sales data feeds more accurate demand planning, helping you align production, inventory, and logistics with real-world performance. This reduces stockouts, excess inventory, and last-minute scrambles that strain cash flow.

Several BI platforms are particularly well suited for food and beverage brands. Crisp is popular with small to mid-sized brands because it connects directly to retailer and distributor portals and delivers near real-time dashboards without heavy set up. For natural and specialty brands already using SPINS data, SPINS ClearCut provides visualization tools layered on top of syndicated data. Larger or more advanced brands often rely on analytics solutions that tie performance data to broader category insights. More flexible platforms like Microsoft Power BI and Tableau can integrate multiple data sources but require more technical set up. For very early-stage founders, even custom dashboards built with Google Data Studio pulling from spreadsheets and distributor reports can serve as a low-cost stepping stone.

The key takeaway is that BI tools are all about clarity. As soon as you're managing multiple SKUs across multiple customers, intuition alone stops being reliable. BI gives you the visibility needed to protect margins, prioritize the right accounts, and plan growth with confidence instead of guesswork.

Start small. In the early days, a well-structured Excel or Google Sheet is often enough. As your distribution expands and promotions become more frequent, graduate into BI tools that integrate directly with retailer portals and syndicated data.

Pro Tip: Retailers and investors love brands that can show data-driven decision-making. Having a BI tool that breaks down SKU- and customer-level performance not only makes your life easier, it positions you as a professional operator in the eyes of partners.

Our Founders' Journey

Elena - Harbor Harvest Foods (Spiced Mango Preserves)

After her first few retail placements, Elena began reviewing her sales reports from each store. Some locations sold through product quickly; others barely reordered. Instead of panicking, she asked questions. Were her jars placed correctly? Were demos consistent? By partnering with store managers and tracking sales weekly, she learned that visibility drove velocity. Small changes, like moving her jars from the bottom shelf to eye level, doubled her turns. For Elena, measurement became empowerment.

Marcus - Summit Sips (Clean Labeled Sparkling Iced Tea)

Marcus had dashboards full of data but struggled to separate noise from meaning. His sales grew, but so did his expenses. After reviewing his reports, he discovered that two SKUs were driving 70% of *Summit Sips'* revenue, while three others barely moved. He made the tough decision to discontinue underperformers, freeing up budget for marketing his top sellers. The numbers didn't just tell him what was happening, they told him what to do next.

Danielle - Bountiful Bites (Upcycled Snacks)

When Danielle finally gathered her financials and velocity reports, the picture wasn't pretty. Her deductions had climbed, her sell-through had stalled, and her trade spend far exceeded returns. But instead of giving up, she brought in a part-time analyst to help her understand her KPIs. For the first time, she could see patterns: her sampling events were effective, but her discounting strategy wasn't. Clarity replaced chaos, and that shift reignited her confidence.

Andre - Kindred Grains
(Ancient Grain Snacks)

Andre had become disciplined about measurement. Every month, he reviewed three metrics: velocity, ACV, and household penetration. When *Kindred Grains* saw a dip in repeat purchase, he launched a retention campaign targeting loyal shoppers through digital ads. Within two months, his velocities recovered. Andre realized that progress wasn't linear, but it was measurable. He was no longer reacting to problems; he was proactively managing performance.

From Promotion to People

By now, you've learned how placement and promotion work hand in hand to move your brand from obscurity to opportunity. You've discovered what it takes to secure shelf space, build relationships with distributors, and create marketing that resonates with consumers in meaningful ways. You've seen how storytelling, data, and execution converge to drive awareness, trial, and loyalty.

But even the best marketing plan can't sustain a company without the right people and structure behind it. Your product might win attention, and your promotion might drive sales, but true staying power depends on your ability to lead, organize, and plan for the future.

That's where *Book Three: Your People and Plan* begins. The final step in the *Kitchen CEO* journey takes everything you've built, the product, the price, the placement, and the promotion, and roots it in a foundation of leadership and long-term strategy. You'll learn how to identify and empower the right team, build internal systems that support growth, and create a comprehensive business plan tailored specifically to the food CPG world.

If *Book Two* was about amplifying your voice in the marketplace, *Book Three* is about ensuring that voice endures. It's about transforming momentum into management, creativity into consistency, and goals into growth.

Your next chapter isn't just about what you're selling, it's about who you're becoming as a founder and leader. With the right people beside you and a plan that reflects your purpose, your brand's potential becomes limitless.

Continuing Your Journey

At this stage, your business is no longer just an idea or a product, it's a brand with the tools to navigate real markets, real partners, and real expectations. As you prepare to turn execution into sustainability, you don't have to do it alone. The Kitchen CEO community exists to support founders as they build structure, systems, and confidence for long-term growth.

Feel free to connect with me on LinkedIn at **linkedin.-com/in/crystalblackdavis**, and to explore tools, guidance, and deeper support at **thekitchenceo.com** as you continue into Book Three.

Sources, Frameworks, and Industry References

Food Industry and Retail Concepts

This book references a wide range of common terminology, operational practices, merchandising concepts, promotional structures, and retail relationship dynamics widely used throughout the consumer packaged goods (CPG), grocery, foodservice, convenience, and retail industries. These terms and concepts are not presented as original intellectual property or proprietary frameworks of the author, but rather as broadly recognized industry language used for educational and informational purposes.

Examples include, but are not limited to:
- Trade marketing and shopper marketing
- Consumer marketing and brand positioning
- Slotting fees and trade spend
- Retail deductions and chargebacks
- Off-invoice allowances and scan programs
- End caps, floor displays, and secondary placement
- Shelf positioning and merchandising strategy
- Retail Media Networks (RMNs)

- Loyalty programs and digital promotions
- Sampling and experiential marketing
- Category reviews and retailer expectations
- Distribution and brokerage relationships
- Pricing tiers and promotional pricing
- Store locator platforms and shopper conversion
- Retail velocity and sell-through metrics
- Planograms, facings, and shelf management
- Co-op advertising and retailer circulars
- Freight allowances and retailer compliance programs

These concepts are discussed throughout the book to help founders better understand the realities of retail placement, merchandising, promotion, and consumer engagement within packaged food and beverage commerce.

Referenced Industry Organizations and Standards Bodies

- Specialty Food Association - Fancy Food Show
- Consumer Brands Association
- FMI – The Food Industry Association
- National Association of Convenience Stores
- Organic Trade Association
- Plant Based Foods Association
- Institute of Food Technologists
- GS1
- U.S. Food and Drug Administration
- United States Department of Agriculture

Business Frameworks and Foundational Concept Sources

Category Management

Retail assortment and merchandising methodologies popularized through retailer-supplier collaboration models developed by The Procter & Gamble Company and Walmart during the modern retail category management era.

Consumer Marketing

Brand-building and consumer engagement principles commonly used throughout modern marketing and advertising disciplines.

Experiential Marketing

Experiential brand engagement concepts informed in part by the work of Bernd Schmitt, *Experiential Marketing.* Free Press, 1999.

GS1 Standards / UPC System

GS1 Global Standards Organization, including UPC and barcode system standards used throughout retail and distribution.

Retail Media Networks (RMNs)

Retailer-owned advertising and digital commerce ecosystems developed throughout modern omnichannel retail environments by companies including Amazon, Walmart, Kroger, and Target Corporation.

Shelf Positioning and Merchandising

Retail merchandising and shelf placement principles broadly utilized throughout grocery and mass retail environments.

Shopper Marketing

Shopper marketing principles and point-of-purchase conversion strategies widely used throughout modern grocery, mass retail, convenience, and omnichannel commerce environments, including frameworks advanced by organizations such as the Path to Purchase Institute.

SmartLabel
SmartLabel Initiative, developed by the Consumer Brands Association and industry partners.

Trade Marketing
Retail and distributor-focused promotional strategies widely practiced throughout the consumer packaged goods industry.

Disclaimer

Certain trademarks, standards, methodologies, frameworks, organizational names, event names, and industry concepts referenced throughout this book remain the intellectual property of their respective owners and are referenced solely for educational, commentary, and informational purposes within the context of the food and consumer packaged goods industries.